10/14/99 NOV 0 9 1999 JUL 2 2 2004
NOV 2 1 1999 MAY 1 0 06
DEC 0 1 1999 APR 1 8 2007
DEC 1 1 1999 JAN 2 8
JAN 18
FEB 2 5 2000
MAR 0 5 2000
MAR 3 1 2000
APR 2 5 2000

SEP 15 1999

My Brother's Farm

REFLECTIONS
ON LIFE,
FARMING, AND
THE PLEASURES
OF FOOD

rother's Farm

Doug Jones

PHOTOGRAPHS BY JAY SAVULICH
POEMS BY GRACE JONES

G. P. Putnam's Sons
New York

We gratefully acknowledge the cooperation of the restaurants mentioned throughout this book for permission to reproduce their recipes. For a complete list of these fine restaurants, please see the Resources section at the back of this book.

G. P. Putnam's Sons
Publishers Since 1838
a member of
Penguin Putnam Inc.
375 Hudson Street
New York, NY 10014

Library of Congress Cataloging-in-Publication Data

Jones, Doug.
My brother's farm : reflections on life, farming, and the
pleasures of food / Doug Jones.
p. cm.
ISBN 0-399-14502-8
1. Cookery.   2. Organic farming.   3. My Brother's Farm (Firm).
I. Title.
TX715.J758   1999
641.5—dc21   98-54599   CIP

Printed in the United States of America
1   3   5   7   9   10   8   6   4   2

This book is printed on acid-free paper. ∞

BOOK DESIGN BY RENATO STANISIC

For my Mom and Dad

CONTENTS

ACKNOWLEDGMENTS

I am, of course, writing this first page last. I've had a lot of fun putting together and writing this book, and a lot of folks helped me out along the way. Although I have practiced my Academy Award acceptance speech a million times, I've never written an acknowledgments before, but here goes.

I'd like to thank all the chefs and restaurateurs who gave me recipes for the book. They're all so busy, and I know that putting together recipes for "Guy's little brother" was yet another thing they had to add to their hectic schedules.

My thanks goes to all the farmers who let me bug them with a lot of questions and who grow all the beautiful produce that Nicolle and I deliver each week.

Thanks also to my family: Guy, Cindy, Ray, Grace, Harry,

Travis, Hayley, Austin, Skyler, and Willa, for their love, their beautiful, enormous personalities, and their hugs and pats.

My brother Guy has helped me pull together the recipes from the restaurants that buy his produce and has answered innumerable questions. Thanks for being the brother in My Brother's Farm.

I'd also like to express my gratitude to: the Katz Brothers—Joshua and my editor, Jeremy—for giving me this opportunity, and reintroducing me to poverty; Jay Savulich of The Grange Hall restaurant for his ongoing assistance and advice; my friends Bill, Ray, Doug, and Eddie, who are always there to encourage and support me in any endeavor; all the My Brother's Farm delivery service clients, especially our longtime customers who have helped us grow; Nadine; and the Malinowskis, who made my first field trip so delightful.

A special acknowledgment needs to be made to my business partner, girlfriend, and best friend, Nicolle Littrell. Her unwavering encouragement is what made this little book possible. She has been my editor, typist, recipe taster, and confidant. Nicolle is the one who takes care of our clients when I forget their tomatoes, who believed I could actually write a book, who makes sure that I don't order carrots three weeks in a row, and who brought me tea while I was writing in our alcove. Thank you, Nicolle, for all your love, support, ideas, and kisses.

Okay, that's it. Hope you enjoy the book!

—Doug Jones

My Brother's Farm

A big mistake is easy. Anyone can make a big mistake. It doesn't take a lot of imagination, no complex plan is necessary. It's also pretty simple to avoid. Don't rob liquor stores, don't tease the lion, don't date the intern, don't order your tea with both milk and lemon. And even if you

THE COPPER FARMER

do make a big mistake, it's easily recognized. "I think I just made a big mistake." Everybody has said it. We all know when a colossal blunder has been made. But a small mistake? A slight error in judgment? A misstep? A lapse? A blooper? A bungle? There's a real art to that.

Much more insidious, too, harder to see. You don't hear a lot of people admonishing themselves with, "Hmm, I think I might have just made a small slip there, whose eventual effect will be revisited on me a thousandfold." And yet, that's how most people accomplish a personal catastrophe. Small mistakes. It worked for me.

I had come home to New Jersey after running away to Taos, New Mexico, where I was a ski bum for a year. I was going to help open a restaurant in New York and re-enter a relationship with a girl my friends referred to as "the disapproving blonde." But she dumped me immediately upon my return, the funding for the restaurant fell through, and I found myself living with Mom and Dad in the New Jersey suburbs. In just a few weeks, I went from skiing in the mornings and playing golf in the afternoons, living in an adorable adobe hut, to sleeping on my old little-boy plastic-sheeted mattress twin bed with a Superman blanket. I was back in my old hometown. I was in shock.

And I was poor. Not the good, free, "the world is my oyster" poor that I was used to from my stint as an aspiring actor in New York City. That was a sort of privileged poor—a young, interesting, happy poverty. That was, "Well, I can't make the rent yet for the month, but I just found thirty dollars in my jeans, so let's go catch the Yankees game."

This wasn't that. This was the "I'm thirty-one, I have no job, and I live with my parents" kind of poor. A ridiculous poor. I couldn't even afford the whole word "poor." "Po." That's what I was. I was po. And unbearably gloomy. My series of small mistakes had marooned me in a beige room right above my parents.

Short on morale, low on options, and out of money, I ended up picking heirloom tomatoes on my brother Guy's organic vegetable farm in Blooming Grove, New York, some thirty miles north of my parents' house.

This was not what I had had in mind when I came back home. I was supposed to be a partner in a groovy restaurant with an adoring and supportive girlfriend at my side. Instead, I was a suburban migrant farmworker with cable TV, occasional access to my dad's car, and no prospects. "Douglas, you pick up that room before you leave this house" had re-entered my life. I had become a thirty-one-year-old migrant adolescent.

As for my social life, well, "Hi, I'm on the rebound, virtually unemployed, and I live with my parents, wanna go halves on a beer?" is not really what the successful suburban single woman wanted to hear.

I was commuting on the ShortLine bus every day to work on the farm, bugging my family for rides to and from the station. I was drinking Yoo-Hoo constantly and eating an enormous greasy egg, cheese, and ham sandwich on a bagel just about every morning.

Eschewing all the beautiful produce on the farm, I instead would go to the Chinese place in Blooming Grove for lunch, where I could get about two pounds of sweet-and-sour anything for four dollars, including egg roll. I had begun to self-medicate my sorrows with those little Oatmeal Creme Sandwich Cookies from Little Debbie. Ahh, Little Debbie. That scamp, that cunning vixen. She had become my secret passion, my guilty delight. I denied myself none of Little Debbie's naughty concoctions. She had a special way with creme, and although I enjoyed her Swiss Rolls, it was for her Oatmeal Creme Sandwich Cookies that I truly loved her. But Little Debbie proved a temporary pleasure, a fleeting distraction. And my steady diet of humble pie was starting to get me down.

Then I found it. My way out of poverty, out of my parents' house, and into my own apartment. Copper.

I found miles of copper wire while I was moping around in a swamp near the farm. A swamp, by the way, is an excellent place to mope, to really get down on life. Any situation in life can be made that much worse simply by relocating it to a swamp. (I was supposed to be out picking wildflowers to sell at the farmers' market, but I've always had a bit of a tendency to wander off.)

It seems that dozens of old utility poles had been cut down along a stretch of railroad tracks when the tracks had been taken out of service. The poles had simply been allowed to drop into the adjoining swamp, copper wire and all. And I had discovered it. It was, I decided, a sign.

Copper was selling for about seventy cents a pound, and there was what looked like tons of it strung about. It was the mother lode of recyclable materials, buried in a smelly swamp.

I abandoned my career as a tomato picker, borrowed my dad's Jeep, and became a copper farmer, pulling the wire out of the hot swamp and coiling it into huge spools. I had to scale a near vertical embankment to get my precious metal out of the swamp. With the spools balanced on a white birch branch across my back, I'd claw my way back up to the tracks, thighs burning, bugs buzzing. I was personally responsible for many generations of mosquitoes having an adequate food supply.

I felt like Bogart in *The African Queen,* trudging through the mire pulling his boat along, but I had no Katharine Hepburn to keep things interesting; just me, Little Debbie, and my wire, though I did see an occasional band of exercising walkers. The tracks were now being used as a sort of fitness trail and a place to ride dirt bikes, which seemed like a curious marriage of mixed uses; power walking to the roar of two-stroke engines.

My sudden appearance on the trail startled quite a few

walkers, as they couldn't see me while I was scaling the embankment. I would stumble out of the high weeds onto the path, filthy and grunting, with my copper wire crucifix balanced across my shoulders. I had to shuffle down the path, a grimy scrap-metal penitent, asking the ladies in their neat walking outfits and tennis shoes to step aside.

I looked like I was making a bizarre pilgrimage to nowhere. Also, for some reason, I had started to dress all in white, as though I was involved in some ancient purification ritual. I wore white pants and a long-sleeved white dress shirt, the collar turned up against the bugs, with a piece of white clothesline as a belt. I had a yellow bandana on my head and a light blue one around my neck, ascot style, a sort of swamp thing meets Truman Capote effect. And I was very dirty.

Sometimes, when the mood hit me, I'd break out singing old spirituals as I trudged along past the power-walking ladies. "Swing low, sweet chariot, coming for to carry me home." Nobody joined in. Thinking back, I don't know why I wasn't arrested.

I shuttled the loads over to the farm and piled them up at the top of the driveway. It was easily the hardest work I had ever done. At the end of the day I would be filthy, exhausted, bug bitten, smelly, and famished, my socks full of mud, my pockets stuffed with empty cookie wrappers. But I was my own boss, and I knew that the harder I worked the more I'd eventually get paid. Copper! My grubstake in the world! A chance to start over, get a place of my own, maybe a little truck, and show that girl who dumped me just how resourceful I was. Move up and move out!

After about ten days of hard labor, I was ready.

I found a junkyard in Jersey City that offered the best price for copper, overloaded my dad's old Jeep, and spent my last three dollars on gas. My brother would have spotted me twenty bucks if I'd asked, but I knew that the junkyard man would be paying me cash for my load.

I'd even called about a little apartment in Waldwick, New Jersey, and I thought I might take a look at it on my way home from my first big commodities deal. I had about nine hundred dollars' worth of copper in the truck, by my figuring. And I had barely scratched the surface of what was lying in that swamp.

I was excited at my prospects. The train tracks went on for miles, with copper wire ripe for the picking. Maybe I could hire a crew to do the grunt work and I could supervise, pass out the Creme Sandwiches, and work on my investments. Maybe even flirt with a passing power walker or two as they marveled at my ingenuity:

"Hello, ladies, lovely day for copper farming, don't you think? Would you care for a Little Debbie?"

Copper farming was my calling. Copper was my way out

of the muck that I had mired myself in. What a break. Suddenly, my future was looking as bright as a copper penny.

Except that it was steel. Steel! With a thin copper coating on it. It was completely worthless. Actually it was less than worthless. The junkyard man put an old greasy magnet against my wire.

"Steel, son. This is steel. Not copper, see?" and then he took a piece of sandpaper and sanded off the thin copper layer to reveal the steel, and my folly, underneath. The look on his craggy face said, "You are a foolish young man, and I pity you." But certainly steel had some value, right? Lots of things are made from steel, aren't they?

"What's it worth?" I asked him, trying to hide my feeling of impending doom.

"Worth?" he snorted. "It's not worth anything. You pay me to take it away. See that insulation on the wire? Well, it's probably got asbestos in it. You can't just dump that stuff anywhere, you know."

You can't?

"I think I made a big mistake," I muttered.

"You think?" he said. "You think you made a big mistake?" And he walked over to the water cooler, just inside the door.

I sat on a spool of my worthless wire on the ground behind the Jeep and put my filthy hands over my face. I slowly shook my head and felt my throat tighten. If you ever get to the point in your life where you find yourself about to weep in a Jersey City junkyard, know that you've made a few wrong turns and it may be time to think about changing course.

The junkyard man returned, with a little paper cup of water for me. I was hoping he had put hemlock in it. He was wise, much wiser than I was, and he hadn't been absent the day they taught which metals are magnetic and which are not, as I evidently was. He had a taciturn quality, that ability to sum a situation up quickly, that many men have whose careers demand that their names be stenciled on their shirts. Like a junkyard Zen master, he knew how to instruct and give advice in a way that I could understand on many levels, even in my sorry state. For I was out past where the small mistakes occur and had entered the realm of the Whopper. I realized that I had become the guy he'd tell a story about whenever a conversation turned to recycling blunders: "One time, I had this guy drive three hours to bring me a pile of old steel wrapped in asbestos, and you know what the first thing he said was? 'So, what's it worth?'"

"This is a tough business, kid," he said, handing me a crisp, clean ten-dollar bill.

"Here, get yourself some lunch," he advised.

"And take all that crap with you."

I knew exactly what he meant.

I reloaded all my carcinogenically coated wire, got in the Jeep, and rested my head against the steering wheel.

"Hey kid," he called, "I'll give you nine hundred for the Jeep."

A test.

My first thought? I was in Jersey City. They practically invented car theft there. It was a perfect alibi for selling my father's car to a junkyard philosopher–opportunist. I mean, if you wanted to get an old, not very valuable car stolen, then Jersey City was the place to do it.

"I was carjacked, Dad. They must have been looking for a beat-up old Cherokee that smells like Aqua Velva and has a broken air conditioner. They target certain cars, I hear."

Or I could use the crime to mask my own foolishness. "I bet they took the car just to get my wire. Copper's going for a lot these days, as I'm sure you know."

But I couldn't do it. It just wouldn't have been right. (Anyway, the title wasn't in the glove compartment.)

Instead, I went home and called my friend Doug out in Chicago. Doug had a "real job," and he and I were about the same size.

"I need you to mail me one of your old suits," I said. "I gotta get a job."

And he did.

And I did.

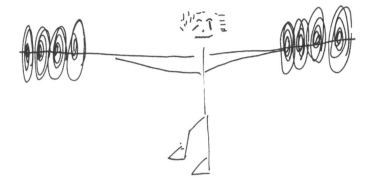

I wrote a résumé loosely based on fact and started going on interviews. The suit jacket didn't quite fit, so I would throw the jacket jauntily over my shoulder when I first went in. I felt that this displayed an air of self-assurance and friendly confidence. And it was much better than looking like your jacket was too small. I did okay on the interviews. Things started looking up on the job front.

It looked like I was soon to be employed, so I decided that it was time I started dating again. So, armed with my tomato money and accompanied by my friend Ray, I started to go out in Manhattan. There are only about fifty-eight single straight men in Manhattan who aren't on parole, so my odds were pretty good.

I met my new girlfriend (and eventual business partner) in an Irish bar on West Fifty-seventh Street in Manhattan.

Nicolle was working at Planet Hollywood, a place that I once worked at as well, before I sort of fired myself. She was out for a quiet after-work cocktail with her friend Kate, who was a friend of mine as well. I shoehorned my way into the conversation.

It ended up that Nicolle had been hired to replace me at the restaurant, and we hit it off quite well. Now, Nicolle is terribly pretty, and I figured that she was most likely dating some fascinating artist, or a captain of industry, or an investment banker, or at least an employed guy. And, although I had been on a few interviews, all I had was the borrowed suit, no job except my tomato gig, and I was carrying my net worth in my pocket. My phone number and my mom's were still one and the same. But Nicolle didn't seem to care about any of that. In fact, she liked the whole farm angle, being an upstate New York girl herself. And she was good luck for me, 'cause right after we met, I got that "real" job.

My brother told me to beware of any job that you've got to buy new clothes for, and ultimately he was right. I told myself that it was only temporary. It lasted three years. But my stint in corporate America was good for me, and it was in my corporate cubbyhole that the idea for "My Brother's Farm Organic Produce and Tasty Morsels Delivery Service" was hatched.

My job was selling temporary help, ironically enough, in

New York City. Each Friday, I would leave the office and go down to the Union Square farmers' market to visit my brother Guy, or my sister Cindy, and my dad. I would bring back a few things each time from Guy's stand for the people at my office. Some tomatoes, maybe a little mesclun, a few bunches of fresh herbs. And then one day, as I was talking with a lady in my office, I was struck by a thought.

"Ooh, Doug, these tomatoes are gorgeous, where did you get them?"

"They're from my brother's farm."

"They're beautiful." And then she asked me, "Where's My Brother's Farm?"

Click. That was it. That was how the idea for My Brother's Farm popped into my head. It's funny how ideas get born.

Nicolle was an actress, and she needed a way to make some dough besides waiting on tables. I needed something to do in addition to finding people crummy temp jobs. And Guy could always use a new way to sell some stuff. We started with a few people in my office as clients. Each week we'd put together a bag of fruit, vegetables, cheese, and bread from the farmers' market. We supplemented what my brother had with produce from other farmers. Everything was locally grown and very fresh. Nicolle suggested that I write a newsletter, and we asked Guy's restaurant clients for recipes. Our delivery vehicle was a taxicab or the subway, and we charged not nearly enough money. But it was fun and we were learning. Then we got our "Public Relations Department" rolling. We delivered a sample bag to *New York* magazine. A small mention in their annual food issue was all it took.

Nicolle and I were vacationing at the Jersey shore when the magazine came out. We got almost five hundred phone calls. We racked up an enormous bill on our calling cards returning calls from a pay phone on the boardwalk. We made so many calls that the phone company kept shutting the cards off because they thought somebody must have stolen them. We went from 20 clients to 120 in a couple of weeks. We were a disorganized mess. But people loved the service and the phone kept ringing.

We were driving all over Manhattan, trying to accommodate everyone's particular schedule. Upper East Side: "I'm leaving for the Hamptons at eleven A.M. Do you think you could be here by then?" Certainly.

The Financial District: "I leave work by noon on Fridays. Can you be here?" No problem. "I'm in the World Trade Center, one-hundred-first floor. You'll need three forms of photo I.D., a blood sample, and a passport to get in. Oh, and can I mail you a check? I'm a little low on cash." Of course.

And the special orders.

"Can I substitute bread for another vegetable?"

"Can I substitute a vegetable for more bread?"

"Can you take out the tomatoes and give me more cheese?"

"I'd like more fruit and no cheese or bread. Can you do that?"

"I'm allergic to peppers."

"I'm allergic to sunflowers."

"I'm allergic to the nightshade family."

"I'm macrobiotic."

"I'm lactose intolerant."

"I'm intolerant in general."

"I'm a vegan. I use no animal products. Do you use manure as fertilizer?"

Well, yes, but we generally don't kill the animal to get its manure, Ma'am. (Although threatening to do so might increase the amount of manure we do get.)

We tried to accommodate as much as we could. (And we still do.) But some of it was impossible. And some of it was nutty. It was trial and error; it was trial by fire. It was trial and trial again.

Eventually, though, we got more organized, thanks mostly to Nicolle. I can't organize a sock drawer, but she did a really great job of systematizing the whole operation. We bought a delivery van and a computer and hired some of our friends to help out. They were all actors, which made for a lot of theatrics at times, but they all worked very hard for us.

And we learned to say no, which was a key to our little company's succeeding.

Our clients seem pretty hooked on My Brother's Farm. We get an amazing amount of positive feedback. And since I'm the one who scribbles it each week, I especially appreciate the comments on the newsletter. Each week it talks a little bit about what's happening on the farm, what's in the bag, coming attractions, and occasionally something about the farmer who grew the food. It is from these newsletters that this book has sprung. Or sprang. (Springed?) I've included some of them throughout the book.

The journey from tomato seed to tomato soup is a surprisingly intricate one, and there are a lot of people involved along the way. My brother, the other small farmers, the farmworkers, the chefs, our customers. All are involved in the food chain of My Brother's Farm. Some of their stories are in here too.

Occasionally, the produce we sell is a little unusual, and we get a lot of "What do I do with this?" questions from our customers. Usually, my answer is "Sauté it in a little olive oil and garlic and squeeze a little lemon on it," no matter what "it" is. Which you could do to the pages of this book and make a passable meal. Just toss with pasta. (It may even make it more palatable.) Anyway, the point is that I've tried to keep the recipes straightforward and simple. Sometimes the professional chefs get a little carried away. They can forget that not everyone has an army of knife-wielding assistants working in a state-of-the-art kitchen, ready to chop on command, and that the home cooks have to have enough time and energy left to sit down and enjoy their creations. At most of the restaurants I've worked at, the chefs are too tired after cooking for anything but French fries, coffee, and beer. Here, though, they've done their best to keep it simple. It shouldn't take you any longer to clean up than it did to eat.

A delivery business of any kind in New York City can be maddening, and a food business particularly trying. The traffic can be unreal (and I could wallpaper my kitchen with the parking tickets). Sometimes a worm will sneak into a piece of corn (ahh, the lure of the big city) and I'll get an earful from one of our clients. Or we might miscount and be long on beans or short on honeydews. But mostly our clients enjoy the service, and we try to put out a product that people will appreciate. Sometimes I still help myself to a nice slice of humble pie, but somehow when you've baked it yourself, it doesn't taste so bad.

One of our customers once said that she could tell that "there's a lot of love in that bag of vegetables." I like that. I hope that some of that spirit spills out of the deliveries and into this book.

SUMMER TOMATO AND GOAT CHEESE SALAD

(UNION SQUARE CAFE)

Serves 4–6

A delightfully simple summer salad utilizing ripe tomatoes and soft goat cheese. If available, low-acid yellow tomatoes make this a particularly colorful presentation, but the salad tastes just as good if you use red tomatoes exclusively. Soaking the paper-thin raw onion slices in water will rid them of their excess pungency and crisp them nicely for the salad.

2 large red heirloom tomatoes

2 large yellow heirloom tomatoes

kosher salt

freshly ground black pepper

1 cup red onions, thinly sliced and
   soaked in ice water

¼ cup basil leaves, thinly sliced

5 ounces fresh soft goat cheese,
   crumbled

4 teaspoons Italian red wine vinegar

¼ cup extra virgin olive oil

Core and slice the tomatoes ¼-inch thick. Arrange the tomatoes on a large platter in concentric circles, overlapping alternating red and yellow slices. Season with salt and pepper to taste. Drain the onions well and lay them over the tomatoes. Sprinkle evenly with basil and crumbled goat cheese.

Season the goat cheese with salt and pepper to taste. Drizzle the vinegar and the olive oil over the salad. Serve.

Sancerre, California sauvignon blanc, and crisp Italian whites are perfect with this tangy salad.

LITTLE DUGGIE'S CREME SANDWICHES

Makes about 16 little heart attacks

First of all, let me say that my version pales in comparison to the original. Creme, especially, is an elusive mistress. It's difficult to capture at home the silken nuances achieved by Little Debbie. But these aren't too bad. Each one, though, is like a punch in the heart, so dole them out sparingly, lest your love of them make your heart actually, rather than figuratively, burst.

THE CREME

6 tablespoons water	½ cup vegetable shortening
2 teaspoons vanilla, the clear kind if you can find it	1 pound confectioners' sugar
	½ teaspoon salt

Beat all ingredients together until smooth. Add the sugar a cup or so at a time, or it will fly all over the place.

Chill the creme while you make the cookies.

THE COOKIES

¾ cup butter-flavored shortening	1 cup brown sugar
½ cup sugar	1 teaspoon vanilla

2 eggs plus one egg yolk

1 cup flour

3 cups rolled oats

1 teaspoon baking soda

½ cup butterscotch chips, softened

Preheat oven to 375 degrees.

Cream together shortening, sugars, and vanilla. Mix in eggs. Mix in everything else. Arrange dough in small clumps on a cookie sheet. Cook till just done, about 9 minutes.

Let the cookies cool completely. Spread one cookie with the creme, and sandwich with another cookie. Wrap them individually and store in a shoebox in the fridge.

My Brother's Farm

JUNE 6

*Now, then, where were we? Hello! And welcome to all of our new clients—and welcome back all you old-timers. Okay, so my prediction of a wild winter was off a bit. Mild, yes. Wild? Nope. And this spring! Ugh. Wet and cold. Plants (and farmers) hate wet and cold—so things are quite a bit behind schedule this year. Hopefully the tomatoes will play ketchup (sorry) and all will be as it should after a few sunny June weeks. Mild winters, though, usually lead to wild summers; we'll see. This winter we bought a new van—well, new to us, anyway. One of those groovy conversion models with leather captain's chairs, a television, and VCR. We're using it for deliveries, so I took the happening chairs and trim out. (We'll leave the VCR, though, for inspirational movies—*The Grapes of Wrath? They Drive by Night?*) *Also, we finally bought a computer. Big one. Does all sorts of stuff. I think. So far, I've mastered the solitaire feature* *and that's about it. Supposedly, though, it will make life easier and billing smoother, will increase productivity, and will add muscle tone. We'll see. The new farm dog, Rosie, who we got to kill woodchucks, has registered five official kills so far this season. Unfortunately, though, they were five chickens, not woodchucks. Oh well, maybe the lack of eggs will lower our cholesterol. Thoughtful pooch. Nicolle and I are happy to be beginning our third season at last and we appreciate your continued support. ☆ We also do organic garden and terrace planting—call for an estimate! ☆ Thanks to all, Doug and Nicolle.*

Eat Your Vegetables *155 Henry Street #5G • Brooklyn, NY 11201*

NINE SPICE ROAST GAME HEN

(THE GRANGE HALL)

Serves 6

3 Rock Cornish game hens	½ cup scallions, chopped
¼ cup fresh thyme, cleaned and chopped	¼ cup dry crushed red chili flakes
¼ cup fresh parsley, cleaned and chopped	½ teaspoon ground black pepper
	2½ tablespoons salt
¼ cup fresh rosemary, cleaned and chopped	¼ cup soy sauce
	1 cup olive oil
	1½ tablespoons minced garlic

Preheat oven to 350 degrees.

Wash and pat dry the hens. With a heavy knife, split the hens along the backbone.

Combine the remaining ingredients and mix well. Coat the entire surface of the hens liberally with the seasoning mixture. Place the birds skin-side up in a roasting pan. Roast 30 to 40 minutes until golden brown. The hens are done when the juice runs clear when the thigh is pricked.

POTATOES SAUTÉED
WITH GARLIC TOPS AND WALNUT OIL

1½ pounds potatoes

¼ cup good walnut oil

*6 six-inch garlic tops, coarsely
  chopped*

fresh pepper and kosher salt

*handful of chopped herbs
  (parsley, rosemary, thyme, etc.)*

Thinly slice the potatoes (skins on) and wrap them in a towel. In a big skillet, heat the oil until hot but not smoking. Add the taters and sauté until browned on both sides—10 minutes a side or so. Add the garlic tops and sauté for just 2 or 3 minutes more. Do not overcook the garlic tops! Sprinkle with the chopped fresh herbs, salt, and pepper. Add a little fresh nutmeg if you like, too. Toss to blend. Serve on our mesclun with bread and cheese and a white Beaujolais and that's dinner.

Have blueberries and vanilla ice cream for dessert. Eat it all.

HUMBLE PIE

5 to 6 good pie apples (I use a
   mixture of different kinds like
   northern spy, macoun, and empire.
   I get them from Chip the apple guy
   at the market.)
1 pint apple cider
cinnamon
a little sugar

2 pie crusts, top and bottom (I
   confess that I often use those
   store-made ones—it is Humble
   Pie, after all—but it's probably
   best to make your own.)
½ cup real maple syrup
1 pint heavy cream

Preheat oven to 350 degrees.

Peel the apples and cut them into pretty thick slices. Soak them in cider for about half an hour. Toss with some cinnamon and a bit of sugar. Put them in the bottom crust. Cover with the top crust. Cut vents in the crust. Trim and reserve the dough that hangs over the edge of the pie tin. Roll out the reserved dough and cut out the word "Humble" with a sharp knife. Spell it out around the crust, attaching the letters with a little water. Wrap a little aluminum foil around the outside edge of the pie so it doesn't burn. Bake for about an hour. Put a cookie sheet on the rack below it. Remove the foil about halfway through the baking.

While it's baking, whisk together maple syrup and the

cream in a bowl. Transfer the mixture to a little pitcher, like a gravy boat. About 5 minutes before the pie is done, pull it out of the oven. Pour the maple cream into the vents of the pie (aahh!) and return to the oven for 5 minutes or so.

This pie is no damn good for you, but it's so tasty. If you don't want to make it "Humble" pie, spell out something else, maybe "Of my eye" (get it? apple of my eye? ugh) or "X the radius squared." Or some other such pi or pie or apple thingy. Folks like that.

RAMPS
BY MY MOM

Nurtured in the streams
of spring,
Reclusive, earthy woodland scamp,
for palates dulled, sweet titillation,
the ramp!

My brother and I are hunting
for his ramp-picking crew on a
cool, sunny April morning. We
follow the deer path next to the
brook that runs from Guy's farm
past the Josephs' property on
Round Hill Road. Across the
brook, the Josephs' place looks
like a golf course, all green

RAMPS

rolling hills. On the water,
there's an escaped Peking duck,
snow white with an orange beak,
flirting with a mallard. The wild
duck flies away, but the domestic
fellow cannot, so he wiggles his
butt at us and heads for the far
side of the creek, quacking crossly.
Last year's dry leaves crunch

underfoot as we look for the picking crew. We come upon a stack of empty yellow lugs, but still no farmworkers. They're all Mexicans now, my brother having pretty much abandoned the hiring of young people who thought it would be fun to work on an organic farm for a season. It can be fun for awhile, but it is extremely difficult, and those seeking a novel experience found that need fulfilled in the first week. Then farming just became hard work.

The shells of freshwater oysters litter the deer path, and I ask Guy if they're edible. "If you're a raccoon they are," he responds. Wild hostas, their leaves a crazy green, flourish in the wet, rich soil. It's not quite a swamp, but the ground is very damp and the creek runs crooked, cold, and deep through here.

A pin-straight row of huge maples, a sugarbush long forgotten, dwarfs the other trees and hints back to this area's agrarian past. Its future, though, is all too evident through the trees: a housing development, its back to the stream. Center hall colonials, bi-levels, also all planted in a row, seem oblivious to the beauty they back up to.

"The stream, these fields, this is why people came here," my brother says.

He wonders aloud why the people who built those houses didn't face them toward the stream, looking out at the Josephs' rolling hills. "They could've put the road in behind the houses," and then, answering his own question, says, "I guess to them, the stream was just something that was in their way."

Still, it's a beautiful spot and the stream runs clear. The ramps are everywhere under our feet. Ramps are a kind of wild leek, a member of the *Allium* family. Raw, they're a bit hard to take, but pickled, grilled, or sautéed, they're unique, spicy, delicious. Chefs in the city, always on the lookout for something "new," have been turning to wild foods a lot lately. Purslane, amaranth, wild spinach, lamb's quarters, and fiddleheads all grow in the wild. Purslane grows in the city, often through cracks in the sidewalk, and people at the market are taken aback when they recognize it and realize that we're charging them four dollars a pound for something that they pull out and throw away.

A few wild foods taste great (especially in the hands of some of the world's best chefs), a few taste like weeds, all of them are great for you, bursting with vitamins and minerals. "Power food" we call them.

The ramps, though, are the best, the most palatable and versatile. I also like fiddleheads, which can make you sick if eaten raw but taste a little like asparagus cooked. Fiddleheads are the first growth of ostrich and cinnamon ferns and grow in the same area as the ramps. Most of the fiddleheads here, though, are too far gone now, sprouting ahead of time after an unusually mild winter. Only the farmers who are farther north have any to bring to market now.

"I don't know where else the crew could be," Guy says.

"Jail?" I offer.

Around here, four Mexicans wielding farm implements in the swamp behind your house is reason to dial 911. "Naa," Guy says. He has secured the tacit permission of one of the homeowners to cut through their backyard and into the woods, but that just grants access to land that neither Guy nor the homeowner owns. The crew has been picked up before, and as the area gets more populated, the gathering of wild foods in spring, as well as leaves for bouquets in fall and pine boughs for Christmas, has gotten dicier. This year, Guy has had to secure permits to gather in areas that he used to go to for free.

"The police pretty much know me now," he says. "And the chief has been pretty tolerant.

"They've been through here already," he says, and I can see little hillocks where the ground has been turned over. "They left a lot behind," I said.

"Yeah, I don't like to wipe a patch out completely, so they'll be here next year."

Guy sees the crew before I do and he lets out a laugh. They're only thirty yards outside of a backyard on the other side of a bend in the creek. They look so out of place, four workers digging in the dirt, filling the yellow lugs up with the green ramps, so close to the backyard toolsheds and above-ground pools. We cross the water on a natural bridge made from a fallen tree. Guy goes across first, and I can tell he's a little anxious to see how they're doing. He makes pretty good money on the ramps, but the season is very short. Another two weeks and they'll be too far gone, too stringy and bitter. This year he hopes to sell two thousand pounds of them at around seven dollars a pound. Not bad.

As I watch him cross the log, I'm struck by how far away Guy is from our suburban New Jersey upbringing, just thirty miles south of here. He's almost fifty, and his blond ponytail swings between his shoulder blades as he balances on the tree. He's at home here in the woods, pointing out different topographies and species of plants, types of trees, and what's good to eat. He admires the old fieldstone walls, the ghosts of the farmers before him, before high-speed travel made this area a suburb, too. Agriculture was not passed down to Guy, but instead it is knowledge he sought out on his own, that he decided he wanted to have.

There weren't really many farms where we grew up, the land long ago became too valuable for that, but lately there seems to be more interest in farming and in natural things in general. Maybe that's why people are interested in the wild foods, because they bring us to another time.

On the other side of the stream, Guy sets the scene: "Stealthily, up from Mexico they come to pick the wild ramps for the crazy gringo farmer."

The Mexicans are speaking quietly to one another, as they are within easy earshot of a yellow bi-level. A conversation in Spanglish ensues between the workers and Guy.

"Near los trees grandes hay mucho," Guy says, pointing to the other bank.

"No hay más here," Ramiro answers.

"How much?"

"Maybe three hundred libras."

I take out my camera, and Ramón jokes, "Maybe you immigration?"

"Sí, my brother trabajo for immigration," Guy jokes.

The men are good-natured, work very hard, and are patient with my bad Spanish.

"Le gustan los ramps?" I ask.

"Oh, sí." They all answer at once.

"Con arroz y carne," they say, "poquito picante."

"Hay ramps en Mexico?"

"Maybe en las montañas," they offer.

They ask me a lot of questions about New York City and the farmers' market and I wish I had paid more attention in Spanish class. How much money do I make on my deliveries? Do other farmers have ramps? Does Guy sell them to any

Chinese restaurants? And the always present question: Are there as many beautiful women at the market as my brother says there are? "Más," I tell them.

The men use a hand shovel and a pitchfork to loosen the ramps from the rich forest soil and stack them neatly in yellow lugs. Later, they'll be thoroughly washed and weighed and Guy will call the restaurants to tell them how many pounds are available. The ramps for market will be bunched. Guy has to get going, so we say our good-byes and I stay behind. Before he leaves, I tell the Mexicans that they're lucky Guy doesn't speak Spanish better or he'd be talking their ears off. They joke that they're going to call Cesar Chavez on Guy because he has them working in a swamp with no "baño" (bathroom), and we all laugh.

"Baño very important," Guy says.

"Oh, sí," says Ramón, "Cesar Chavez love el baño." Ramp picking is better than the fieldwork on the farm, the workers tell me. Not so hot, "no hay muchos insectos."

They graciously pose for a group photo as I wait for the flash to power up on my disposable camera. "Más juntos," I tell them. "Closer." I tried to give Ramiro directions to the other ramp patch Guy and I saw, but I don't think I was very clear.

I wish I could see what I'm actually saying in Spanish to these guys, that there were subtitles running under our conversations. My Spanish vocabulary is so limited and I get the meanings all mixed up. Once, at a barbecue, I walked up to Ramiro and told him I was a lawn chair and I said that the meat was having good weather. I'm sure that they think I'm nuts. A little knowledge truly is a dangerous thing.

It's time for me to get going, so I say good-bye and grab a few handfuls of ramps for dinner. They smell green and cool. I follow my brother's path back across the log bridge and out of the woods, cutting through the backyards back to my van.

PICKLED RAMPS

(GRAMERCY TAVERN)

1 pound ramps, cleaned and
  trimmed

½ cup sugar

1 cup water

1 cup white wine vinegar

1 tablespoon mustard seed

1 bay leaf

1 sprig thyme

1 tablespoon cardamom

1 tablespoon fennel seed

Bring a large pot of water to a boil. Blanch the ramps for 1 minute. Drain and cool under cool water. In a medium mixing bowl combine the remaining ingredients. Add the ramps and allow them to steep for 1 week in the refrigerator. Before using, bring the pickling mixture and ramps to a boil. Remove from the heat and cool.

Serve as an accompaniment to roasted meats or grilled fish.

RAMP AND MINT PESTO

(HOME)

Ramps are wild leeks and appear on hillsides throughout America in the early spring. Here in New York we see them in April and May. They are smaller and more pungent than the cultivated leeks and have a hot peppery garlic flavor. We like to make pesto with them using the whole ramp. This pesto can be used like ordinary pesto as an accompaniment to just about anything. Our favorite way to serve it is with roasted leg of lamb.

1 pound ramps, cleaned, blanched,
  and roughly chopped
2 cups basil leaves
1 cup mint leaves
2 tablespoons garlic

1 cup toasted pine nuts
2 cups olive oil
1 cup grated Parmesan cheese
salt and pepper

In a food processor, puree the ramps, basil, mint, and garlic. With the food processer still on, add the pine nuts and process until smooth. Continue to process and slowly drizzle the olive oil into the paste until it is incorporated. Add the cheese and season with salt and pepper.

PURSLANE AND FIDDLEHEADS
WITH FRESH HERBS

½ pound fiddleheads
¾ pound baby carrots
8 small cipolline onions,
* quartered*
2 cloves garlic, minced
½ pound cremini mushrooms
½ pound baby fennel, bulbs cut
* lengthwise, fronds reserved*

⅓ pound purslane
1 cup vegetable or chicken broth
a little butter for sautéing
fresh thyme, mint, Italian parsley,
* and basil*
salt and pepper

Boil the fiddleheads in salted water until just tender, about 4 to 5 minutes. Take them out of the water. Plunge into ice water to keep them nice and green (the fiddleheads, that is, not you). Pop those carrots into boiling water for 2 minutes. Take 'em out and drain on paper towels, or the preceding page of this book. Now drain those fiddleheads, too. Sauté the onions, garlic, mushrooms, fennel bulbs, carrots, and purslane in a little butter. Add them one at a time in the order above. Don't stir them around too much, and use a high heat so you get some caramelizing. Add the broth. Now add the fiddleheads, the fresh herbs, and a few snips of the fennel fronds. Lower heat and sauté until the fiddleheads are just warm. Add salt and pepper to taste. Put it in some bowls, and cut up some nice bread to go with it.

This is an extremely healthy and tasty way to eat some weird vegetation. Serve with chicken fried steak, nondairy whipped topping, and blubber.

Soft Polenta with Asparagus, Prosciutto, Garlic, and Ramps

(PO)

Serves 4

5 cups water

1 pound large asparagus

1 cup polenta

1 cup mascarpone cheese

6 tablespoons butter

3 cloves garlic, thinly sliced

3 slices prosciutto, julienned

12 ramps, cleaned and root ends
  removed

juice and zest of 1 lemon

½ cup dry white wine

Set up an ice bath.

Place 5 cups of water in a 4-quart saucepan and bring to a boil. Trim asparagus and cook until tender, about 1½ minutes. Remove and refresh in the ice bath. Return the same water to a boil and, whisking constantly, pour polenta in a thin stream until all is incorporated. Remove whisk and stir with wooden spoon until as thick and dense as Cream of Wheat. Remove from heat. Fold in mascarpone and let stand.

In a 12- to 14-inch sauté pan, heat 4 tablespoons butter over medium heat until foaming. Add garlic, prosciutto, and ramps and sauté until ramps are wilted. Add asparagus, lemon juice and zest, and white wine, and bring to a boil. Add remaining butter, shake pan to emulsify, and season with salt. Divide polenta among 4 bowls, top each with asparagus-ramp mixture, and serve immediately.

I was, for a year, a vegetarian. The girl I was dating was one, so I became a sort of "come with" vegetarian, a vegetarian by association. It seemed fitting that I become one. My brother was a vegetable farmer, after all. I like vegetables well enough, and I was

BE A VEGETARIAN . . . OR JUST LOOK LIKE ONE

interested in losing a couple of pounds. What I became, though, was a cheeseatarian. I had a cheese monkey on my back. "Can I get cheese on that?" became my mantra. "Large pizza, extra cheese, please" should not be in your working vocabulary if you're trying to lose weight. But as a cheeseatarian, I was hooked. I needed that cheese fix. Fettuccine Alfredo with extra cheese, cheese and crackers, cheese fries, nachos with cheese, mozzarella sticks, cheese and chocolate fondue. Yellow cheese, blue cheese, green cheese, white cheese.

In restaurants, I was a terror. "Give me any vegetable you got back there. I don't care what it is. Just deep-fry it, slather it with cheese, and bring it to me. But no meat! I'm a vegetarian! Are you? Well, don't you want to be? Don't you know that a single steak stays in your colon for eleven years? No thank you! No meat for me, I say! Hey! Where ya going?"

I bought a MEAT IS MURDER bumper sticker. I felt guilty about my leather shoes. I vowed never to eat anything with a face. (Except for those big delicious cookies at the bakery on Ninth Avenue.)

"I'm a vegetarian" worked its way into virtually every conversation I had. It made no difference what the topic was, I could somehow turn it to a point where I felt "I'm a vegetarian" was an appropriate comment. I had become the unbearable vegetarian. The righteous, unbearable vegetarian.

I was also like a spokesmodel for unhealthy vegetarians everywhere. In a year, I gained eleven pounds. I was proof that it takes very little effort to avoid meat and still manage to eat like an idiot. Breakfast? Cap'n Crunch with Crunchberries. Lunch? Peanut butter, American cheese, and Fluff with a milkshake. Dinner? A pizza with French fries on it (still a favorite) and maybe some nachos and beer after work. But no meat! I'm a vegetarian! A vegetarian! Do you hear me?! And I'm okay with it! It's fine! It's just fine! It's great and I love it! I'm also left-handed. I'm a left-handed vegetarian. And I'm fat, yes fat, and angry! I'm a fat, angry, left-handed vegetarian! Now give me a piece of cheese.

I returned to my carnivorous ways the day that relationship ended. The very hour, actually. We broke up and I went directly to the Film Center Cafe on Ninth Avenue and had a big steak. They served it with broccoli, which I did not eat.

I guess I never fully embraced my vegetarianism. I was always seeking out something to substitute for meat, rather than simply accepting that you could live just fine on vegetables alone. It's sort of like converting to the metric system. If you keep on trying to remember how much something would've been in inches, instead of just accepting how long it is in liters or meters or whatever they use, it's impossible to ever fully adopt the new way of life. Eating Not Dogs just made me yearn that much more for a good old hot dog (or a "dirty water dog" as they're called on the streets of New York).

When I got the contract to write this book, my editor offered to take me out for lunch to celebrate. "Anyplace you want to go, just name it," he said.

I was feeling good. My first book contract. A city full of restaurants. I wanted something classic, a New York institution. Where would Hemingway have gone?

"How about someplace 'manly,'" I suggested. "Someplace where we can get a big steak and have a martini and talk about women and football (two topics I know nothing about). Someplace where we can be manly men, someplace like Smith and Wollensky's Steakhouse," I suggested.

A pause on his end.

"What's wrong?" I asked. "Too expensive?"

"No, it's not that," he said. "It's just that, well, I'm a vegetarian."

FRICO DI PORTOBELLO
CON PATATE E CIPOLLE

(FRICO WITH PORTOBELLO AND POTATO-ONION FILLING)

(FRICO BAR)

Serves 4

2 medium-large baking (Idaho)
    potatoes (about 1 pound),
    unpeeled, scrubbed
4 tablespoons extra virgin olive
    oil
½ cup onion, sliced thin
½ cup leeks, white and green parts,
    washed well and cut into ½-inch
    rounds
salt and freshly ground black
    pepper

4 large portobello mushroom caps
    (about 1½ pounds), stems removed,
    brushed clean and brown gills
    scraped off
4 garlic cloves, crushed
1 sprig fresh rosemary
1 pound Montasio cheese, rind
    removed, coarsely shredded (about
    5 cups)
tender young salad greens, washed,
    dried, and dressed

In a pot large enough to hold them comfortably, cook the potatoes in boiling salted water until tender, but still firm—the skin should be unbroken—about 25 minutes. Drain the potatoes and let stand just until cool enough to handle.

Peel the potatoes and cut them into ¼-inch-thick slices. In a large skillet, heat 2 tablespoons of olive oil over medium heat. Add the onions and leeks and cook, stirring occasionally, until wilted, about 4 minutes. Add the sliced potatoes and cook, turning the potatoes gently occasionally, until golden, about 8 minutes. Season with salt and pepper.

Meanwhile, in a large skillet sauté the mushroom caps in remaining 2 tablespoons of olive oil with 4 garlic cloves and rosemary. Cook for 10 minutes over medium flame. Season with salt and pepper.

Preheat the oven to 250 degrees.

Fricos can be done individually and kept warm or done in multiple skillets. I would recommend doing two at a time. Place a 2- to 5-inch nonstick skillet over medium-low heat until a shred of the cheese begins to sizzle 2 to 3 seconds after it hits the pan. Scatter about ⅓ cup of the cheese in an even layer over the bottom of the skillet. Arrange ¼ of the potato-onion filling over the cheese and press it very gently into an even layer. Set a portobello cap on top, press gently, and sprinkle another ⅓ cup of cheese over the filling in an even layer. Let the bottom layer of the cheese cook without disturbing it or moving the pan until the fat that separates from the cheese begins to bubble around the edges, about 3 minutes. At this point shake the skillet gently to free the cheese crisp from the bottom of the pan. If it sticks, let it cook a minute or two longer, then try again. If at that time the crisp is still sticking in places, carefully work a heatproof rubber spatula under the crisp to free it. In about 6 to 7 minutes total cooking time the underside of the crisp should be an even golden brown and the crisp should slide very easily in the pan. Slide the crisp onto a small plate, then invert the crisp back into the skillet. Cook the other side as you did the first. Slide the crisp out onto a baking sheet and keep it warm in the oven while cooking the remaining fricos. Pat dry with a paper towel, cut in half, top with dressed greens if you like, and serve.

To cook filled fricos on a griddle: Heat a cast-iron or other heavy, stick-resistant griddle over medium-low heat until a shred of the cheese begins to sizzle 2 to 3 seconds after it hits the surface of the griddle. Using ⅓ cup of the cheese for each, form as many circles, about 4 inches in diameter, as will fit on the griddle without touching. (If this is your first time making filled fricos, you may want to make slightly smaller fricos on the griddle; they will be easier to flip.) Fill and cook as described above, simply flipping the crisps with a metal spatula when the underside is golden. Filled fricos cooked on a griddle will require about 12 minutes total cooking time.

These recipes are from an excellent restaurant in Manhattan, Angelica Kitchen. It also happens to be a 100-percent vegetarian restaurant, and their food is delicious. You don't need to be a vegetarian to appreciate this food. If I ever do venture down the vegetarian path again, I'll eat more like this.

PHYLLO CASSEROLE WITH POTATOES, BEETS, AND SPINACH

(ANGELICA KITCHEN)

Serves 4 to 6

1½ pounds yellow-flesh potatoes,
  peeled or unpeeled
1 pound beets
4 cups onions, thinly sliced
2 tablespoons garlic, minced
2 tablespoons fresh oregano, minced
  (or 1 teaspoon dried)
2 tablespoons extra virgin olive oil
2 tablespoons fresh lemon juice,
  strained

2 pounds fresh spinach, washed and
  large stems removed
sea salt to taste
freshly ground black pepper to taste
8 ounces phyllo dough
½ cup canola oil, for brushing phyllo
  and pan

Steam the potatoes until tender. Pressure cook for 15 minutes or boil beets for 45 minutes to an hour, or until tender.

Preheat the oven to 400 degrees.

Sauté the onions, garlic, and oregano in olive oil for 8 to 10 minutes, or until soft. Mash the potatoes along with the garlic and onions; set aside. Cool and peel the beets under cold running water; cut into ⅛-inch-thick rounds. Toss with lemon juice and set aside. Steam the spinach until just wilted. Cool in a bowl of cold water, squeeze dry, and chop. Season with salt and pepper to taste. Oil a 10-by-10-inch Pyrex pan. Layer 3 sheets of phyllo, lightly brushing with oil between each layer. Spread potatoes evenly over the phyllo. Spread the spinach over the potatoes; layer the beets over the spinach. Cover the casserole with 10 sheets of phyllo, each sheet lightly oiled.

Bake for 30 minutes or until golden brown. Serve with Garlicky Braised Lentils and Dill-Tofu Sour Cream.

GARLICKY BRAISED LENTILS

(ANGELICA KITCHEN)

Yields 6 cups

1 cup French lentils, sorted and
   washed
6 cups water
6 whole cloves garlic, peeled
1 whole bay leaf
1 teaspoon fresh thyme, minced
1 teaspoon fresh rosemary, minced

2 tablespoons extra virgin olive oil
1 tablespoon mirin
2 teaspoons red wine vinegar
sea salt to taste
freshly ground black pepper to
   taste

Combine lentils, water, garlic, bay leaf, thyme, rosemary, olive oil, and mirin in a heavy-bottomed pot. Simmer gently for 40 minutes or until tender. Add vinegar, salt, and pepper to taste.

DILL-TOFU SOUR CREAM

(ANGELICA KITCHEN)

Yields 2½ to 3 cups

1 pound firm tofu

¼ cup fresh lemon juice, strained

⅓ cup canola oil

1½ tablespoons fresh dill, finely
  chopped

4 teaspoons rice vinegar

1½ teaspoons sea salt

¼ teaspoon white pepper

Combine all the ingredients in a food processor fitted with a steel blade, and process until creamy.

VEGETABLE LASAGNA
WITH CARROT-BEET SAUCE

(ANGELICA KITCHEN)

Serves 8 to 10

1 pound whole wheat lasagna
  noodles

Carrot-Beet Sauce (recipe follows)

filling (recipe follows)

Tofu Ricotta (recipe follows)

Preheat oven to 350 degrees.

Bring 4 quarts of water and 1 tablespoon of sea salt to a boil, turn off the heat, and soak the noodles for 5 minutes. Drain.

Spread 1 cup of Carrot-Beet Sauce in the bottom of a 9-by-13-inch lasagna pan. Cover the sauce with a single layer of noodles, slightly overlapping. Spread half of the filling over the noodles. Top with a single layer of noodles. Spread the remaining ½ cup of sauce over the noodle layer. Spread the remaining filling and then the final layer of noodles. Spread the Tofu Ricotta on top.

Bake for 1 hour or until the ricotta is light brown and firm. Allow the lasagna to rest for 10 minutes before serving.

CARROT-BEET SAUCE

Yields 2 quarts

1½ pounds onions, peeled and diced
¼ cup olive oil
1½ pounds carrots, peeled and diced
2 cups beets, peeled and diced
2 tablespoons garlic, peeled and
  minced
1 quart water

3 tablespoons fresh herbs (thyme,
  tarragon, sage, basil, or rosemary),
  finely chopped
2 tablespoons red wine vinegar
2 teaspoons sea salt
freshly ground black pepper to taste

In a heavy 3-quart saucepan, sauté the onions and olive oil over medium heat for 7 to 8 minutes. Add the carrots, beets, and garlic to the onions. Lower the heat and cook, covered, for 30 minutes, stirring occasionally. Raise the heat and add the water and herbs. Bring to a boil, lower heat, cover, and simmer for 20 minutes. Puree until smooth while adding the vinegar. Add salt and pepper to taste.

FILLING

2 quarts mushrooms, wiped clean
   with a damp towel, and sliced
8 tablespoons extra virgin olive
   oil
1 tablespoon sea salt, plus more to
   taste
1½ pounds onions, peeled and diced
2 quarts greens of choice (kale,
   collards, or mustard greens),

washed, chopped, and firmly
   packed
1 pound tempeh, cut into
   ½-inch cubes
3 tablespoons tamari
1 cup olives, pitted and chopped

Preheat oven to 425 degrees.

Toss the mushrooms with 2 tablespoons of oil and 1 teaspoon of sea salt; spread on a cookie sheet and roast for 30 minutes.

Meanwhile, sauté the onions in 3 tablespoons of oil and 1 teaspoon of sea salt over medium heat for 8 to 10 minutes, or until lightly browned. Steam the greens in a steamer basket over high heat for 6 to 8 minutes, or until tender. Remove and chop finely.

Spoon tempeh and roasted mushrooms into a large mixing bowl. Add the tamari, onions, greens, and olives. Toss well and add salt and pepper to taste.

Tofu Ricotta

1½ pounds firm tofu, rinsed and
  patted dry
6 tablespoons canola or olive oil
2 tablespoons fresh herbs (tarragon,
  basil, thyme, or rosemary), finely
  chopped

1½ teaspoons sea salt
⅓ cup fresh lemon juice, strained
freshly ground black pepper to taste

Combine all the ingredients in a food processor fitted with a steel blade, and puree until smooth.

Yukon Gold Potato, Carrot, and Granny Smith Apple Soup

(THE GRANGE HALL)

Yields 2 gallons

6 carrots, washed well and diced

½ gallon leeks (approximately 15 medium), white part only, trimmed, rinsed thoroughly, and diced

2 ounces canola oil

12 cups water

5 ounces Minor's Sautéed Vegetable Base*

12 Yukon gold potatoes, peeled and diced

5 Granny Smith apples, peeled, cored, and diced

8 teaspoons coriander seeds

1 teaspoon ground black pepper

5 bay leaves

In a stock pot or a large heavy pot, sauté the carrots and leeks in the oil until tender. Add the water and bring to a boil. Stir the Vegetable Base into boiling liquid until dissolved. Add the remaining ingredients and return to a boil. Reduce heat and simmer until vegetables are tender (approximately 30 minutes). Remove the pot from the heat and discard the bay leaves. Allow the liquid to cool slightly, then puree ingredients in a food processor until smooth. Return to the pot and check seasoning. Reheat if necessary, and serve hot.

*You can get Minor's Vegetable Base by calling 1-800-243-8822.

GREEN GAZPACHO

(VERBENA)

2 tablespoons sugar

¼ cup water

2 medium cucumbers

4 medium tomatillos

15 fresh basil leaves

2 tablespoons champagne vinegar

2 tablespoons chili oil or olive oil

Tabasco or cayenne to taste

salt

1 red pepper, diced

watercress

Dissolve sugar and water in a small saucepan, about 2 minutes. Remove from the heat. Peel and chop the cucumbers into 1-inch pieces. Remove the husk and rinse the sticky surface of the tomatillos. Cut into quarters. In a blender, blend cucumbers, tomatillos, basil, sugar syrup, and vinegar. Finish with chili oil, Tabasco, and salt to taste. Garnish with small dice of red peppers and watercress.

MAIL-ORDER BUGS
BY MY MOM

An "insectary" sounds rather scary!
But not to little bugs;
It's a training school where they are taught
to chomp on bad-guy slugs.
Ladybugs and lacewings and
mantises that pray
Will attack those vicious villains
gobbling hungrily each day.
These good guys of the critter world
save gardeners in distress,
arriving with their legs-a-lot
via Mail Express!
And busily they go to work
on the save-the-veggies scene.
Mail-order bug crusaders
Help to keep the garden green!

I've got 24,000 bugs in my refrigerator. I ordered 18,000 ladybugs, 5,000 green lacewings, and three praying mantis egg cases, containing about 200 little praying mantises each, from Bio-Control Network. These critters are what's known as "beneficial insects," bugs who eat up or chase

MAIL-ORDER BUGS

away bad bugs. Beneficials are a way to manage pests without resorting to chemical sprays. And you can order the bugs right out of a catalog, just like J. Peterman or Victoria's Secret. Except the models are leggier. It feels a little odd to be opening a big box of mail-order bugs in my Brooklyn living room. Usually people are trying to get bugs *out* of their Brooklyn apartments. I gently pull back the cardboard flaps, wishing I had a backyard to be doing this in. Apparently the folks who sent them to me know what they're doing, and everything is neatly packed. With delivery and tax, they cost $77.50, which seemed pretty cheap to me, given the sheer number of little souls involved, and I confess that I immediately thought of all the practical joke possibilities of mail-order bugs.

The bugs arrived via overnight Federal Express from an insectary in Arizona. "Insectary" is a marvelous word that I had never heard before, but that instantly conjured up a creepy mental picture of multitudes of slimy bugs and bug eggs, larvae, and pupae, of a building full of squishy, crawly things.

Which also describes my bug-infested first New York City apartment on West Forty-fifth Street in Hell's Kitchen. I wish I had known that word when I lived there. I would've had a little plaque made up for the door, "Welcome to 410 W. Forty-fifth Street. The Insectary." That apartment had a comical amount of cockroaches in it. And they had a lot of personality. They must have been in cahoots with the rental agent, because they were nowhere to be found when I looked at the place, but they were everywhere once I moved in, sharing my food, reading my newspapers, spelling out words on the wall, and occasionally feasting on my eyebrows at night. (Really!)

I shot off a few of those room foggers to get rid of them, but that just made them giddy. I tried roach motels, but they already had an apartment, what would they want with some dingy motel? Then I tried the more organic approach. At the farmers' market, they sell a weird-looking green, inedible fruit called an "osage" orange that's supposed to give off an odor that repels cockroaches. Osage oranges are about the size of a grapefruit with wrinkled chartreuse skin. I bought dozens of them, at two for a dollar. I should have known I was in trouble when the farmer asked me, "So, what are you going to do with all these?"

"What do you mean what am I going to do with them?" I replied. "I'm going to use them to repel cockroaches."

"Okay," he said. "Just seems like you're buying an awful lot of them."

"You should see my apartment," I said.

They didn't work, of course. The roaches just scurried around them like they were gates on a slalom course. But my apartment was now full of these strange green globes. It looked like an avant-garde art exhibit, the little chartreuse bocce balls strewn strategically about the floor. Very Martha Stewart, in a Hell's Kitchen kind of way.

I could hear the roaches chuckling as they rolled them

around at night. And the farmer and his wife must've laughed all the way to the bank. "Earl, get those damn green things out of the driveway, they stink." "Hey honey, let's tell those crazy city people that these here stink balls repel cockroaches. Those New Yorkers are so naive, they'll buy anything. But we need a fancy name, it's all marketing these days, you know."

We will buy anything, it's true. After all, I had just invited eighty dollars' worth of bugs into my new apartment, after spending hundreds to rid my old place of uninvited guests. It's good to keep in touch with your roots, even if your roots are crawling with aphids.

The little darlings I purchased had been in a sort of suspended animation in a refrigerator out there in sunny Arizona, but when they got to me, they were wide awake.

The ladybugs smelled pretty bad, as 18,000 of any little creature would. And they made a pretty gross noise, crawling all over each other, their little hard shells clattering together. They arrived in a net bag, about the size of a quart of milk. That's how they're sold, in fact, by the quart. And they were trying very hard to get out. A creepy huddled mass, yearning to be free.

A single ladybug crawling about outside in the garden is cute. Little black dots on her pretty red shell. But 18,000 ladybugs crammed in a bag is a little weird. I'm pretty sure that when that box arrived, I possessed more ladybugs, lacewings, and praying mantises than anyone else in Brooklyn. A dubious honor, I reckon. (My friend Ray called just after I had put the bugs in my refrigerator, and I exclaimed, "Hey Ray, I've got over twenty thousand bugs in my fridge!" "Are you complaining, Doug, or are you bragging?" he deadpanned.)

The lacewings are shipped as eggs packed in bran cereal, which I'm sure the bran cereal people would be happy to know about. What a product endorsement: "High in fiber, and larvae love 'em!" Perhaps they chose bran to keep the little wrigglies regular. They would be much easier to see if they packed them in Froot Loops. Unfortunately, it was very hot the day I ordered the lacewings, so a lot of the eggs hatched before they got to me. This means that instead of a little vial of bran flakes and tiny white eggs, I received a vial of crawling little lacewing larvae. It looked like the cereal had come alive. A vile vial. A closer look revealed that the little critters were happily eating the bran flakes, and each other. My 5,000 eggs were about to yield one fat lacewing cannibal with a high-fiber diet.

The praying mantis egg cases looked like three little balls of papier-mâché, each a bit smaller than a golf ball. They were very light for their size, and delicate-feeling. Each little globe had 200 little praying mantises in it. Luckily, there were no signs of life yet, and I stuck them right in my own fridge, next to the milk, those bran flakes, and the ladybugs.

I thought that I had better call the bug guy, because my bugs looked like they were ready to bust out and I wasn't scheduled to release them for two more days.

"Just observe the bran flakes for a few seconds, you might see some of them move," Eric from Bio-Control said.

So I sat there observing bran flakes. After what I saw, I think I'll be observing all my bran flakes a little more closely.

"You'll see either green, white, or gray little eggs. Or you may have many larvae crawling around at this point."

"Oh yeah, I've got larvae, and they're eating each other."

"Yeah, they do that," he said calmly. "You'd better let them out."

"Now?"

"Well, soon. By tomorrow," he advised.

"So I can't let them just live in the bran flakes till Monday, then?"

"No, you'll have to put them out. They will eat each other," he said again.

"How about the praying mantises?" I asked. "Are they going to hatch in my refrigerator? It wouldn't make me very popular."

"No, they shouldn't. They need a few days of eighty-degree weather to hatch."

No, they shouldn't? That's all the reassurance I get?

"And the ladybugs? How long can I hold on to them?"

"Oh, they'll keep a couple of weeks," he said cheerfully, like a proud papa. "Just sprinkle them with a little water, they'll keep."

"They smell a little funny."

"Yeah, they do that," he said.

My head was starting to itch.

In East New York, Brooklyn, there's a community garden behind an assisted-living center where I help out sometimes. I helped the therapist who runs the garden, Katie, put in an herb garden, and Nicolle and I buy the herbs for our delivery customers. It works out pretty well. They get a chance to make a few bucks to cover garden expenses, and we get extremely local produce. An assisted-living center is a place where people are trying to get their lives together and learn how to get over addictions. The garden is a nice refuge for the living center's clients.

A lot of the younger kids from the neighborhood like to hang out in the garden with Katie. It's pretty amazing to see how quickly these city kids take to growing things.

Because it was the garden's first season, there were no real problems with pests (besides me). But I thought it would be a good idea to get some beneficial insects established there before any bad bugs from the neighborhood started hanging around. And East New York seemed like the kind of place where there would be a lot of bad-bug types about. East New York has more than its share of everything that's wrong with a big city: drugs, crime, bad housing. But right in the middle of it is this little garden, and the herbs, tomato plants, collard greens, and flowers that were planted are doing great.

This garden was where I would be releasing the bugs I bought. We had to push up the release date by two days, since the bugs were ready to go. What a shock for them. Sleeping peacefully in a refrigerator in Arizona one day. Then a cross-country flight, probably a red-eye, nervous with anticipation: "Hey! We're going to New York City! Maybe we're going to Central Park, the Brooklyn Botanical Gardens, or the Bronx Zoo!" Only to land at La Guardia Airport, wind up in my living room, and then be released in one of the most notorious neighborhoods in town. Poor little buggers.

I wanted the kids to get a chance to meet the bugs before we released them, so Katie had arranged a little ladybug party, with ladybug stick-on tattoos and cupcakes, and Nicolle and I brought some watermelon, strawberries, and 24,000 insects—everything you need for a swell little picnic.

We thought we'd give each kid some ladybugs and a spoonful or two of the larvae in bran to set loose in the garden.

I had a terrible picture in my head of me portioning out

to each kid a mound of the bran flakes to sprinkle about the garden, and then some little kid popping the cereal in his mouth. (Got milk?)

When I was ordering the bugs, I asked Eric the bug guy if he had any larger bugs I could buy, ones the kids could see easier than the little larvae packed in bran flakes. Something they wouldn't be tempted to eat.

"Sure we do," he said. "We've got some enormous crickets, which I could let you have cheap."

Even mail-order bug salesmen like to haggle, it seemed. "Crickets?" I asked. "Are they a beneficial insect? Do they help out in a garden?"

"No," he replied, "not at all. They'll eat anything. But then next year I could sell you the bug that eats cricket larvae."

Everybody's working an angle. This guy was trying to sell me a plague of locusts so next year he could sell me pestilence remover. No thanks, Moses. Hey, how's the market for frogs, gnats, and flies doing? Got any of those staffs that turn into an asp lying around? Any ideas on how to part the Hudson?

Really, though, Eric was very helpful. He also pointed out that I hadn't ordered any of the "Good Bug Power Meal," which sounded so healthy when I read the catalog description that I wished I had a little for myself to sprinkle on my bran

flakes in the morning: "14 amino acids, 8 vitamins, nitrogen-free extract, lactose, and sucrose. For your beneficials."

"Just sprinkle some baby formula around the garden for the adult insects to eat," Eric advised. "It's a pretty similar recipe. That way the adults will stick around more."

"Okay, I'll do that. Thanks, Eric," I said, and I went

across the street to buy the bugs baby formula at the super-market. When I got home with my little can of formula, I realized that Eric had probably meant the powdered kind, not the liquid that I bought, but I felt too ridiculous to call him up and ask him which kind of formula his ladybugs pre-ferred. I just went back over to the store and bought the right kind, too. The cashier gave me a knowing, "you dumb male" kind of glance. "So you got the wrong one, huh?" she said.

"Yeah," I said, "I got the wrong kind. I guess the little buggers eat it dry."

The kids took to the ladybugs like bees to spilled lemon-ade. I couldn't shake the bugs out of their bag fast enough. They weren't squeamish at all. The ladybugs, too, seemed pleased to be out.

"One of them is up my shirt!"

"I've got one on my neck! It tickles!"

"They're not going to bite me?"

"Hey, one flew!"

"How come you're letting all these bugs out here?"

"Put some in my hand."

"Mine flew too!"

"That one likes me."

"Look, Miss Katie, I got one on me!"

"I want to bring some bugs home for my mom." (Wouldn't that make *me* popular with the local moms.)

Bio-Control should be selling these things as party favors, the latest trend in the "can-you-top-this" world of kiddie birthday parties. The Insectary Party.

Seven or eight kids and 18,000 ladybugs is just about the right ratio. They had a great time setting them free around the garden, sprinkling them on the collards, the tomatoes, and the sunflower stalks. They did a good job putting out the lacewing larvae in the bran flakes, too (and nobody ate any).

We put one praying mantis egg case in a box so the kids could see them after they hatched. We put the other two cases in the crotch of a tree, ate some cupcakes, had a little watermelon, and listened for the exodus of the bad bugs away from the neighborhood. A little garden is a powerful thing.

My Brother's Farm

212 615-6733 *Support Your Local Farmer*

JULY 13

*Summer's heavy hitters, step up to your plates this week. Basil
leaves first, taking a long lead and daring to get picked off. The
wizened old veteran, Red "Heirloom" Tomatoes, is in the number 2 hole, having another excellent season, acting so young and
fresh it looks like he's still growing. And Corn, who had a slow
spring but is now in midseason form, what a sweet swing!
Somebody stop me. Those odd little pods with the papery jackets
you got there? Those are husked tomatillos. Take their jackets
off (it is summer after all) and pop them in your mouth.
Strange, but good (like love). They grow on a bush that grows
about a foot off the ground and are very tough to pick (like
lovers?). They're worth working for (sometimes it seems
everything means two things). And those tomatoes? Those are
"heirloom" tomatoes, so don't eat them, just pass them down to
your children along with the hope chest and the season tickets.
Actually, they're called heirloom because they're older varieties
that aren't commonly grown on a large scale anymore. See,
tomatoes now are chosen because they're tough and can handle*

the arduous journey to market from California or Florida or Ohio. That's a great way to pick a tire, but a lousy test for a tomato. The heirloom types sometimes look a little bizarre and misshapen, but they have excellent taste. Sort of the Bela Lugosi of tomatoes. Some of you will get "Green Striper" tomatoes. They're ripe now. They don't turn red, so eat 'em up.

We were on TV last week. Did you see us??? The Food Network followed us around for a few hours, which was strange, but good (like husked tomatillos). We're selling the movie rights. Bela Lugosi plays me, Nicolle plays herself. Hey!! People! Recycle. We're stuffing your pantry full of those big ($.40!) shopping bags every week. It'd be swell if you left the empties with the doorman every week so we could swap you full for empty. Some of you already thought of this (thanks, Mildred). Hey Florence and Laurence, your doorman wanted basil for his pesto, so we gave him a bunch this week. He seems like a nice fellow. Time to go, early start tomorrow. It's gonna be hot! Play ball! Thanks all.

Doug and Nicolle

Toasted Wild Rice Salad with Quince, Walnuts, and Dried Cranberries

(Knickerbocker)

4 shallots, peeled and diced

2 medium carrots, peeled and diced

1 ripe quince, peeled, cored, and
  diced

1 cup wild rice

3 cups vegetable stock

¼ cup chopped toasted walnuts

¼ cup dried cranberries

walnut oil

sherry vinegar

salt and pepper

In a large saucepan over medium heat, sweat the shallots, carrots, and quince with a small amount of oil, just until tender. Add the rice and cook for 5 minutes, stirring occasionally until it is toasted brown and smells nutty. Cover with stock and turn heat down to a slow simmer. Allow to cook 25 to 30 minutes. The rice is finished when the sides of the grain crack, exposing the white inner flesh. You may need to add more stock to reach this point. When the rice is done you may also need to pour off excess liquid. Stir in the walnuts and cranberries, dress with oil and vinegar to your taste, and season with salt and pepper. Serve warm. This is a great side dish for turkey.

GOAT CHEESE AND BEET SALAD WITH ARUGULA AND BALSAMIC VINAIGRETTE

(KNICKERBOCKER)

2 large beets

6 ounces goat cheese

salt and pepper to taste

8 ounces arugula

3 ounces Balsamic Vinaigrette

(recipe follows)

Place the beets in cold water and bring to a boil. Continue boiling until their skins rub off easily. Remove from the heat and allow to cool. Peel and slice the beets into ¼-inch slices. Soften the goat cheese to room temperature in a small bowl using the back of a spoon. Season with salt and pepper. Trim off the long stems of the arugula and wash thoroughly. Spin dry. Distribute the arugula evenly on 4 salad plates. In a large mixing bowl combine the beets, goat cheese, and vinaigrette. Using your hands, mix the ingredients together, and serve over the arugula.

BALSAMIC VINAIGRETTE

2 ounces balsamic vinegar

1 ounce Dijon mustard

salt and pepper to taste

4 ounces olive oil

Whisk together the vinegar and mustard. Season with salt and pepper. Slowly drizzle in the oil while whisking.

Nicolle and I live near the Promenade in Brooklyn Heights. The Promenade is a wide pedestrian walkway built onto the edge of the Heights, overlooking the East River. It's built over the Brooklyn-Queens Expressway and offers spectacular views of the

MY BROTHER'S BROTHER'S FARM

Manhattan skyline. The Promenade is lined with park benches, and there's lots of pretty gardens behind wrought-iron fences. People walk dogs, push baby strollers, and sit and read or contemplate the view. The beautiful Brooklyn Bridge is off to the right, and, just left of center, the Staten Island ferry sets out from the tip of Manhattan.

During the day, workers from the nearby offices dine al fresco, balancing deli sandwiches on their laps, and sodas on the slanty benches. Kids ride their bikes, groups of tourists take snapshots of the view, and there's a lot of hubbub about.

At night, there's a different vibe. Lovers kiss and eat ice cream, and old folks go for a little stroll.

Manhattan is all lit up, the taillights stream across the bridge, and I can feel the hum that is the energy of New York. The Promenade is a great spot. But the Promenade and the expressway cut off a slice of Brooklyn, the piece closest to the river. This little strip of land is only a few hundred yards wide. It's about seventy-five feet below the height of the Promenade and it's a bit of a mess. Old abandoned piers and warehouses, mostly. And one vacant lot, stuck between a Port Authority building and a Metropolitan Transit Authority electrical substation.

I decided that it would be fun to farm that little plot, so I did a little digging and found out who the owner was, or who it appeared to be, according to City Hall, anyway. The owner listed is a large real estate holding company in Manhattan. I wrote a letter to the president, whose name is Vincent, and followed it up with a phone call.

He was very nice about the whole subject and seemed to

like the idea. He said he needed a week to research it. In the meantime, I went down and checked out the lot.

It's a pretty good size, almost an acre. But it was a mess. There's an eight-foot-high fence all the way around it, but this being Brooklyn, there was a big hole cut in it. Some homeless people had been hanging around down there, and there was a lot of garbage around. I dug a few holes to check out the soil, and although there was a lot of broken brick and some wire in it, it wasn't too terrible. There were some earthworms, and the land was supporting a pretty healthy crop of weeds. I didn't find any two-headed crickets or a huge patch of five-leaf clovers or anything, but I though it might be good to get the soil tested. The results, after seventy-five dollars, were that there were some contaminants from the expressway exhaust and that the soil contained lots of brick and wire. So often it seems that experts merely restate the obvious.

I called Vincent back at the end of the week. Of course, there was a problem.

"Well, I don't know if I own it," he said.

"What?" I asked. "What do you mean?"

"Well, I know we used to own it, but I don't know if we still do," he said.

I felt like saying, "Oh yeah, I forgot, here it is, I own it. Sorry to trouble you."

I found this pretty amazing. I knew this company owned

a lot of property, mostly apartments and commercial buildings, but how could they lose track of three-quarters of an acre on the Brooklyn waterfront? Did the little card slip under the board? Did he trade it for the green ones, or a red hotel on Baltic Avenue? I suggested to Vincent that maybe he might want to drive by the property (he could hop in his little metal shoe or saddle up the terrier). But he said he knew where it was.

"It's a knockdown," he said. Sounded technical.

"What's that?" I asked, displaying my ignorance.

"Uh, there used to be a building on it that got knocked down."

"Aahh. Right. A knockdown," I said, sounding ridiculous. Well, that explained the brick and wire.

He was very patient with me. Finally he said, "Look. I can't give you permission to go ahead, but I'm not going to stop you. And you might have a problem with the bums there, you know. There's a fence around the place, but they'll just cut a hole in it."

"How do you think I'm getting into the property now?" I said. He laughed.

"Look, put your own lock on the fence and be careful. If you can pull it off, you ought to get a medal," and then he hung up.

And that, I figured, was as much of a stamp of approval

as I needed or was likely to get. I called my brother and asked for advice. He was very helpful, but after he told me all that would need to be done, I was a bit daunted. I decided to lower my sights a bit and just concentrate on the back half of the property.

The first job would be to clear the land of garbage and weeds. Then I would roll out black plastic, cut out spots to seed through, and till only where the seeds went in. The plastic would keep the weeds down, and this method would keep tilling at a minimum. This was important, since my only tool was a hoe I bought at Sears.

I had mixed feelings about clearing the lot of garbage and then covering it with strips of plastic, but there was no other practical solution. I decided I would plant wildflowers and sunflowers on the unused front portion of my "farm."

Guy lent me his Weedwacker, and I got to work. This is no ordinary Weedwacker, though. No little fishing line spinning around. This thing has teeth and would just as easily become a toe whacker if I wasn't careful. You have to wear this harness-type thing with it, so that it's attached to your body (I forgot to bring the harness the first day, so I looped my belt around the machine, a bad idea). And since it has a gas engine, it gets hot and really loud. I felt like I was wearing a Volkswagen. But it whacks the weeds, all right. It took about eight hours to clear the back half, and it felt great.

Occasionally, I would look out toward the East River and New York's massive skyline beyond. What an amazing place to grow flowers! And how beautiful it will look from up on the Promenade. As I was unstrapping myself from the machine, I looked up at the Promenade and saw a bunch of folks admiring the view. It was a pretty good crowd. Then a few of them waved to me and I waved back. I imagine it must've looked a bit odd. Some nutbar with his belt wrapped around an enormous Weedwacker, his conversion van parked nearby, clearing a vacant lot on a desolate strip of Brooklyn waterfront. But that's one of New York's most incredible qualities—the level of tolerance for the out of the ordinary. I mean, I could dye my hair pink and ride a hippo down Broadway and nobody would really care all that much. "There's a pink-haired guy on a hippo. Gotta get to work." I do hope, though, that people will stop and smell the flowers, if I can coax them out of the ground.

The seeds I ordered cost $94.86. Cosmos, bachelor buttons, zinnias, three kinds of sunflowers, and mixed wildflowers. I was surprised by how much sunflower seeds are, almost $9.00 for a quarter pound. Sunflower seed for birds is about $2.00 for five pounds. I'll have to ask what the difference is. Or try planting birdseed. So far I have cleared out eight bags of garbage, including one hundred and thirteen empty Thunderbird wine bottles (an incredible display of brand loyalty!), seven sneakers, two shopping carts, eleven hubcaps, thirty-four iced tea bottles, five traffic cones, an overcoat, and a cat (not alive). I have laid out six forty-foot rows, four feet wide, three feet apart.

Brooklyn used to be full of farms, and at some point way back when, this little spot was probably under plow. It's very therapeutic to till the soil and guide a few seeds to maturity. But there's a long season yet to go, and there's still a few problems to solve. I need to figure out how to get water to the flowers. There's a hydrant right out front, so perhaps I can ask the local firehouse for a little help. The birds seem to love the wildflower seed I planted, so I'll need to keep an eye out for them. I wonder what other little creatures I'll meet. And I have to fix that hole in the fence. Also, I may be trespassing. I wonder if Vincent will lend me his "get out of jail free" card. It's still early spring, the project is just getting started. Realistically, the best results will be seen next year. But a flower or two on this ground will be a big improvement.

BAKED ROMA TOMATOES

(SAVOY)

12 Roma tomatoes

2 teaspoons cumin seed

1 teaspoon coriander seed

2 teaspoons black peppercorns

2 teaspoons red pepper flakes

1 tablespoon sweet paprika

½ teaspoon cayenne

2 teaspoons sugar

3 teaspoons salt

olive oil

Preheat oven to 250 degrees.

Slice the tomatoes in half through the stem and place, pulp facing out, on an oiled sheet tray. Set aside.

In a small skillet, warm the cumin and coriander in the oven for 5 minutes, then combine with the peppercorns, pepper flakes, paprika, cayenne, sugar, and salt in a spice grinder and process until fine.

Drop 1 teaspoon of olive oil on each tomato and sprinkle with a pinch of the spice mix.

Bake until the tomatoes are wrinkled slightly, about 60 minutes. Remove and let cool 10 minutes before serving.

PUMPKIN SFORMATO WITH FONDUTA AND FRISEE

(BABBO)

Serves 4

1 pound wedge of pumpkin

2 cups Balsamella Sauce (recipe
  follows)

4 egg yolks

2 eggs

¼ cup plus 2 tablespoons freshly
  grated Parmigiano Reggiano
  cheese

¼ cup fresh bread crumbs

½ cup milk

4 ounces fontina cheese, grated

1 head frisee lettuce, washed and
  spun dry

1 ounce extra virgin olive oil

½ ounce red wine vinegar

Preheat oven to 375 degrees.

Wrap the pumpkin in foil and bake 1 hour. Remove and cool. Cut pumpkin into 1-inch cubes and place in a mixing bowl. Add Balsamella Sauce, yolks, eggs, and ¼ cup Parmigiano, and stir together. Lightly butter a Bundt pan and dust with bread crumbs. Pour the batter into the Bundt pan and place in bain-marie. Place in oven and cook for 1 hour 15 minutes, or until a toothpick stuck in center comes out clean. Allow to cool.

Meanwhile, heat milk over low heat until foam forms. Add fontina and 2 tablespoons remaining Parmigiano and stir to combine. To serve, slice into 1-inch pieces. Place on plate with dressed frisee and drizzle with the fonduta (cheese mixture).

BALSAMELLA SAUCE

4 tablespoons butter   *1 cup cream*

4 tablespoons flour   *salt and pepper*

1 cup milk

Melt the butter in a skillet. Blend in the flour. Remove from heat and slowly add liquids; blend till smooth.

Return to the heat and cook slowly, stirring constantly, until the sauce is thick and smooth. Season with salt and pepper.

SOFTSHELL CRABS WITH A SALAD OF HEIRLOOM TOMATOES, SPRING ONIONS, SPRING GARLIC, AND AGED BALSAMIC VINEGAR

(CUB ROOM)

Serves 8

2 pounds assorted heirloom tomatoes

1 bunch spring onions, sliced paper thin

1 bunch spring garlic, sliced paper thin

salt and pepper

5 tablespoons extra virgin olive oil

8 jumbo-sized softshell crabs (Ask your fishmonger to clean them for you; otherwise, you'll have to remove the gills, face, and tail ends.)

Wondra flour (a very fine-milled flour)

1 bunch basil leaves, about ¼ cup, julienned

3 tablespoons aged balsamic vinegar (the older the vinegar, the better the end product)

Slice heirloom tomatoes and arrange on a platter. Sprinkle onions and garlic over tomatoes. Season with salt and pepper. Drizzle with olive oil, but don't put the vinegar on until you are ready to serve them.

Dry the crabs on a towel and season with salt and pepper. Dust with Wondra flour. Sauté in olive oil about 3 minutes per side until golden brown. Place them on a towel after sautéing. Place the crabs on top of the salad. Garnish with basil. Drizzle the crabs and salad with balsamic vinegar, and serve.

OYSTERS
BY MY MOM

There is moisture
in an oyster
especially dipped in butter.
There is silence, deep dark silence,
'cause a word it does not utter.
But they are oh, so very busy as they
swim and dip and swirl,
for those smart and tasty bivalves
are just jewels at making pearls!

If you're going to be an oyster (and
you never know), Fishers Island,
New York, would be a great
place to be one. It's like an oyster
spa. You'd spend your first year in
an oyster nursery, in a saltwater
pond overlooking a golf course.
Then, assuming you survived,

FISHERS ISLAND
OYSTER FARM

you'd be one of the most pampered
oysters in the country. After your
year in the nursery, you'll be
culled and cleaned and suspended
in baskets from a long buoy line
in a protected cove, just
offshore from some pretty pricey
real estate. You'll have regularly
scheduled power washes, and

you'll even get to bask in the sun on occasion, lazing around on the edge of a dock. No starfish will be able to crack you open, the birds won't be dropping you onto rocks, and you'll constantly be getting checkups to make sure you're fit and healthy. Your every need will be anticipated and met. You'll be fresh, young, and you'll want for nothing (a sort of trophy wife of the bivalve world).

And, during that time of year when you start to feel amorous toward that certain special oyster who shares your basket, the "do not disturb" sign will be hung on your buoy line, leaving you free to do what comes naturally.

Not a bad life for an oyster. Of course, your last few days will be spent packed in a cold, dark, cardboard box before you're slathered in hot sauce, drizzled with lemon, and eaten alive at some tony New York restaurant, but life is a series of trade-offs, especially if you're an oyster.

"We're sort of like a microbrewery for oysters," explained Steve Malinowski, the owner of the Fishers Island Oyster Company. "We sell about four hundred thousand oysters a year, and every one of them passes through my hands a couple of times."

I asked Steve how many of the 400,000 had passed through his lips, and he smiled. "The kids eat them, sometimes, but I don't eat too many. I'm usually too busy to open them up, plus when I think of how much work goes into them, I'd rather sell them."

Like a skinny chef, this made me a little distrustful. I'd kind of figured that he'd be eating oysters willy-nilly, breakfast, lunch, and dinner. Or that he'd be able to recite a litany of oyster recipes, like Bubba the shrimper in *Forrest Gump*. But Steve's oysters do enjoy a stellar reputation among New York restaurants. And he must be eating some of them, because the Malinowskis are a living tribute to one bit of oyster lore: They have five children.

Fishers Island is technically a part of New York State, but its lifelines are more tethered to the Connecticut coast than to New York. The island sits about four miles off the mainland. It is beautiful, not overly developed, and its coves lend themselves well to aquaculture. It's best, though, to show up on the island with a big bag of money and all your stuff, because the real estate isn't cheap and there's only a couple of stores, so whatever you don't bring, you probably won't be able to buy on the island.

I had arranged to meet Steve's wife, Sarah, at the marina in Noank, on the Connecticut coast, at 7:30 A.M. A couple of their kids wanted to go to a bigger school than the one on the island, so they attend a school on the mainland. Happily, the Malinowskis have friends whose children prefer the smaller island school, so Sarah drops off her kids by boat and picks up their friends' children for the ten-minute Boston Whaler ride back to the island. It was via this school shuttle that I would get to Fishers Island.

The previous afternoon, I sat at the bar of the Seahorse Tavern at the marina in Noank and had a beer and some delicious fried clam bellies. I had no idea just what a clam belly was, but the word "fried" has always been among my favorites, so I jumped right in. The bar was full of local contractors: the painters, electricians, and carpenters that populate every seaside area, ribbing each other and buying one another beers.

I asked the bartender if it'd be okay to park out front for the day tomorrow. She opened the question up to the committee at the bar. No one thought it'd be a problem, and they seemed to wonder why I had even bothered to ask. Noank is that kind of place—laid back, quiet. Asking a parking question had probably marked me as a city person in their eyes, an outsider, and I didn't feel like feeding any of these wise guys a straight line as good as "Just what is a clam belly, anyway?" so I left the mystery intact. I figured the answer would appear to me at the right time.

"Going out on the water tomorrow?" a house painter asked me.

"Yeah," I said, "I'm going out to Fishers Island to talk to an oyster farmer."

"Your rig will be fine out there."

"Sure," a carpenter agreed. "No one will bother it. Besides, there's more parking spaces than bar stools, anyway." Which seemed like irrefutable logic.

A pause, and then another fellow grinned and asked me, "So, got any nice tools on the truck?"

The next morning, I parked in my spot outside the Seahorse (locked the doors) and walked down to the water. It was a beautiful sunny May day with a light breeze and low humidity. I met Sarah at her friend's dock. Sarah is outdoorsy-looking, pretty, and fit. We hopped in the Whaler school bus and sped off toward Fishers Island. During the ten-minute ride, Sarah told me how she and Steve had first started with raising clams, and then did a lot of shellfish research projects for various government agencies before settling on oyster farming. Later, Steve explained that the first decision they had made was that they wanted to live on Fishers Island, and then they had to figure out a way to support themselves there. The oysters were the means to that end. The Malinowskis have recently moved into a pretty house on a little bluff overlooking a small, quiet cove. In the cove are a couple of docks stacked high with lobster pots, a few small sailboats, and one

commercial dock, for marine supplies. The houses on the
water are lovely, well spaced, not all jumbled up like too
much of the Atlantic coastline.

"It's a constant struggle to maintain the island's charac-
ter," says Steve on a quick tour of the island. Steve is about six
feet three inches tall, with broad shoulders and rugged good
looks. Actually, the whole Malinowski clan—Steve, Sarah,
and the five kids, ages twelve to eighteen—look like they
stepped out of the pages of a J. Crew catalog. The girls are tall
and pretty, and the boys have strong, handsome features and
good builds. (Maybe it's the salt air.) And they all seem like
nice kids, too. They're funny. And they're athletic. They're
smart. And they live in a beautiful place. And the Malinowskis do interesting work. And they're their own bosses.
They even have a nice old dog who woofs agreeably, and a
picnic table under a shady tree. They're redoing their new
house themselves, and it looks great. Bugs seem to circum-
vent their yard. I'm sure that their leaves probably blow down
to their neighbor's place in fall. The whole thing would be
unbearably irritating if the Malinowskis weren't so pleasant
and unassuming. They are the Rockefellers of oysters.
(Sorry.)

The island is seductive in the lifestyle it offers. There are
less than 250 full-time residents. The population expands to
about 4,000 during the summer, and the majority of the year-

round folks are contractors working for the summer people in one capacity or another. The locals need the summer people but don't always love what comes along with them. I remark on what looks like a pickup truck culture on the island. "Yeah," Steve replies, "but that's become a bit of an issue," a phrase I will hear a couple of times on my visit. Steve explains, "It doesn't cost much to bring your car over on the ferry from New London, and it's cheaper than parking it back there, so everyone brings their cars. But they don't like to drive them on the unpaved roads, so more of the roads get paved, which means even more traffic, and runoff when it rains, too."

The population during the summer has increased the pressure on the island's tiny infrastructure as well.

"Years ago, people had summer homes here, and when they weren't using them, most of them were just left empty. Now, though, people look at a home here as an investment, and they rent them out whenever they're not using them, no matter how much money they have."

The Malinowskis don't sell their oysters on the island. "That was a conscious decision on our part," Steve says. "We don't want any part of our success to be dependent on the further development of this island." They do, he said, do a bit of bartering with friends on occasion. Somehow, the idea of paying for something with oysters seems very agreeable to me.

We pass through the center of town, which consists of a post office, a school, the firehouse, and a couple of "shoppes."

"We've got a couple of shoppes now," Steve points out, and I can tell from his tone that he feels that this is development enough, that a couple of shoppes is as much of a tourist industry as he wants for the island. He seems to use the word "shoppes" to differentiate these establishments from an actual "store," where useful things are sold. There's an ice cream shoppe, a dress shoppe, and an antiques shoppe. A movie theater shows films three times a week during the summer. There is one store on the island, selling food, beer, newspapers, and a very good homemade poundcake, as well as some local lobsters. There is one bar as well.

Inside the store, we meet up with a local woman, and she and Steve discuss the impending restart of the Millpond 2 nuclear power plant in Connecticut. Back in the truck, he explains: "Part of the island is within the ten-mile radius of the plant, so we have to have an evacuation plan."

The plan, concocted by the government for the island, is for those within the ten-mile radius to drive a few miles to the north end of the island, which would put them farther than ten miles away but still stuck on the island. This seems ridiculous, considering that the place is only seven miles long. ("The poor Smith family. They all perished from the fallout. But we were perfectly safe. If only they'd crossed the street like the rest of us.") It's pretty hard to get far enough away from something like a nuclear reactor accident when you live on an island. And the congested Connecticut coastline seems like an odd place to build a nuclear reactor in the first place.

Steve's passion for the environment is obvious on my visit, especially when it comes to his oysters. "It's more important for us than anyone else on this island for the waters here to be clean."

The Malinowskis have the oysters tested once a week for a variety of bacteria and have never had any problems. "The bacteria (*Vibrio vulnificans*) that makes people sick is much more prevalent in the warmer Gulf coast waters than up here," he says. "It's definitely more of a problem down there, but we test for it just the same."

Although Steve doesn't sell his oysters in June, July, or August, eating oysters in the summer is more a question of taste than of safety when it comes to Fishers Island oysters. "American oysters, when they reproduce in the summertime, it's not as nice a product. They get a little milky inside and don't have as good a flavor." And what about that tradition of not eating oysters in months without the letter "R"?

"That might come from before there was refrigeration," Malinowski explains. "It would've been difficult to ship them in the summertime. Also, some of that came from Europe, too. The European oyster, the Belon oyster, spawn during the summertime and they brood their young (carry the young inside their shells), unlike American oysters. So it's almost like they have sand inside them, if you eat them when they're brooding their young."

Eating some critter while it's brooding its young will probably never become a big culinary craze; it's just too gross ("our special tonight is a mommy possum that was brooding its helpless young when we fried it in a light egg batter"), to say nothing of the somewhat unpalatable fact that you'd be wiping out an entire generation of little European oysters with each bite. The Malinowskis' oysters take the summers off to fatten up.

Steve is also a doctor of marine biology in addition to being an oyster farmer. "There is a little science involved in the hatchery part, but the grow out is pure muscle." He laughs. "We don't have anything mechanized, very low-tech, with lots and lots of lifting."

We are standing in his hatchery, a long low building that is a converted dog kennel. It is immaculately clean. On one wall are about a dozen backlit Poland Spring five-gallon water bottles glowing with green liquid. It's oyster food for the baby oysters, which are contained in two large vats. Right now, they're only about as big as raspberry seeds. With the filters bubbling away and the dim green-hued light, the hatchery looks like Aquaman's workshop. The smell is pleasant, sort of like bacon mixed with the beach. The beach part is obvious, but maybe the bacon is of my own conjuring, or perhaps I'm daydreaming about clams casino or something. Anyway, the hatchery is where the oysters get their start. It is also where their ultimate fate is determined; the front half of the hatchery is the office where Steve contacts his restaurant clients and fills his orders.

"I have to do all of the final packing. That's really what makes our product unique. Making the decision on which oysters go in the box and which ones go back in the water is critical. I also interface with all the customers myself as well."

In this way—the literal hands-on approach—Steve reminds me a lot of my brother's attitude about mixing his mesclun. They have to personally be involved in the selection and packing of the final product. This guarantees a high level of quality but limits their ability to grow.

"What I like to do is the day-to-day work involved in raising the oysters rather than pounding the streets of Manhattan selling them and being an administrator, so we've actually scaled back from a high of six hundred thousand oysters to the current four hundred thousand or so." Which still leaves plenty of grunt work.

"We've had a few days where me and one other person

moved over one hundred thousand pounds between us, all by hand."

We take a small, flat-bottomed workboat out to the cove where the oysters hang in large baskets suspended in the water from buoy lines. Steve is dressed in bright-orange rubber overalls so he doesn't get wet when he lifts out the oyster baskets. The movement of pulling up an oyster basket is an awkward one. You have to reach down below your feet and snatch the basket out of the water, pull it onto the edge of the boat as the water drains, and then jerk it onto the boat's floor. It looks like a procedure designed in a marketing class for chiropractors. My back hurts just watching him do it, but he handles it easily.

The basket has a little seaweed growing on it. Steve checks the oysters for mussels, which will grow right on top of the oysters if given the opportunity. The seaweed, too, can be a problem, limiting the water flow to the oysters in the basket and creating an environment for other critters to grow. Like any other farmer, pest management is a vital part of the job. Any mussels would be power-washed off. The seaweed is killed by letting the baskets sit in the sun on the dock for a little while, which sounds pretty simple. But it means that the baskets have to be hauled up out of the water, lifted up onto the dock, and then hung back out on the buoy line again once the seaweed is dead. Each basket is pulled out of the cove and put back in a minimum of five times during the season. Also, finding a place to put out the buoy lines can be difficult.

"We have a permit from the town, the state, the Army Corps of Engineers, and the Coast Guard. People don't want to look at the buoy lines, and our marine environment is traditionally for recreation. In other countries, aquaculture is more tolerated. Here, some people don't like it that you're using the ocean as a business. One of the major challenges to aquaculture in this country is finding a site to do it. There are coves on this island that would be perfect for an operation like ours, but it's hard to get permission."

The people who own the home directly in front of Steve's buoy lines appreciate the nautical look of the buoys in their bay and don't have a problem with him floating them there. They do add something to the look of the bay, and are a testament to the cleanliness of the waters here.

Although he is extremely gracious and patient, I can tell that Steve is not entirely comfortable with having me traipse along with him and pepper him with questions as he goes through the routine of his day. Plus, some of my questions are just dumb, I realize, once I hear his answers. ("Any problem with zebra mussels here, Steve?" I ask, dredging up some mussel factoid I'd stored for just this moment. "Um, no. Those are a freshwater mussel, Doug, and this is saltwater." Yup, it certainly is, what with it being the ocean and all.) Also, he doesn't seem thrilled that I keep taking his picture. But he has a good sense of humor and puts up with me and my fancy new camera that I don't really know how to use.

Most farmers are somewhat loners, and I suppose this is especially true of one who has chosen to live on an island. But they do like to talk once you get them going, and like many others of his breed, Steve is passionate about his work and his environment. It's obvious that he enjoys his job and is proud of his family.

Today's shipment of oysters, one of the last of the season, is packed in insulated boxes. They'll ride the ferry over to New London, where the UPS truck will pick them up and chauffeur them to swanky restaurants in Manhattan. ("Good news: You get to go to every fancy joint in town. Bad news: You're an oyster.")

I say my good-byes and hitch a ride back to Connecticut with one of the Malinowski boys. He talks about his upcoming trip to Europe this summer. The Whaler passes the buoy lines, and the Malinowskis' new house sits on the hill overlooking their cove. Steve and Sarah wave good-bye from their dock. They seem to realize that the world is their oyster, with an "R" in every month.

Oyster and Winter Vegetable Chowder

Yields 2 quarts

4 tablespoons vegetable oil

4-ounce piece of bacon, trimmed
   and cut into 4 chunks

6 leeks, washed and sliced thin

1 stalk celery, cleaned, trimmed, and
   sliced thin

½ onion, peeled, sliced thin

1 quart chicken or vegetable stock,
   or water

1 pound potatoes, peeled, quartered,
   and sliced thin

4 ounces white wine

8 ounces water

24 oysters, scrubbed

4 ounces turnips, peeled, quartered,
   and sliced thin

4 ounces cream (optional)

2 tablespoons chopped parsley

Place 2 tablespoons oil and the bacon in a pot over medium heat; render the bacon until lightly browned. Add ⅔ of the leeks and the celery and onion, and cook, covered, on low heat until the vegetables are tender, about 7 minutes. Add the stock and half the potatoes to the pot and bring to a boil. Simmer until the potatoes are tender. Puree the soup base in a blender until smooth, and reserve.

While the base is cooling, bring the wine to a boil in a pot; add the water; return to a boil, and add the oysters. Cover the pot and steam just until they open. Strain oysters, reserving the oyster juice. When the oysters are cool, shuck them and cut the oyster meat in half; reserve.

In a pot on low heat, add 2 tablespoons oil. Add the remaining leeks (whites only) and potatoes, and the turnips to the pot, and cook until tender. Add the pureed soup base and oyster juice and bring to a boil. If using cream, add and bring back to a boil. Add the oysters. Stir in parsley, and serve.

PAN ROASTED OYSTERS
WITH CHEESE PUMPKIN SAUCE

(CUB ROOM)

Serves 6

Cheese pumpkins are the best variety for cooking. They're also called sweet milk pumpkins. They're available at groovy food stores or farmers' markets.

36 oysters

sea salt and freshly ground pepper

Wondra flour (Wondra is a very
  fine-milled flour)

3 tablespoons olive oil

Cheese Pumpkin Sauce (recipe
  follows)

fresh chervil sprigs

Shuck the oysters. To shuck, remove them from the shell and detach the muscle. Reserve oysters in their juice until you are ready to cook them, then remove oysters from juice and dry on a towel. Reserve the juice. Season the oysters on both sides with fine sea salt and freshly ground pepper, and dust with Wondra flour. Sauté the oysters in olive oil in a hot pan until they turn golden brown.

Strain the reserved oyster juice into the Cheese Pumpkin Sauce. Be careful of pieces of shell. Pour the sauce into 6 shallow bowls and arrange 6 oysters per bowl. Garnish with fresh chervil sprigs.

Cheese Pumpkin Sauce

2 pounds cheese pumpkin, cut into
   chunks and seeded
2 teaspoons cinnamon
⅛ teaspoon fresh nutmeg

2 tablespoons honey
1 tablespoon butter
salt and pepper
1 quart water

Preheat oven to 400 degrees.

Place the pumpkins in a baking dish and season with cinnamon, nutmeg, honey, butter, salt, and pepper. Pour water into the baking dish, cover with foil, and bake for 45 minutes to an hour, until the pumpkin is soft. Scrape the pumpkin into a saucepan and whisk in the baking liquid until smooth. If there is not enough liquid, add more water and seasonings from above to make smooth. Bring to a boil, adjust seasoning, and pass through a fine mesh sieve, making sure to push through as much pumpkin meat as you can. Keep warm.

CRACKER MEAL FRIED OYSTERS
WITH TARTAR SAUCE

(PEARL OYSTER BAR)

1⅓ cups all-purpose flour

⅔ cup cracker meal

*16 oysters, shucked (Reserve curved
   shells for presentation. Wash
   thoroughly.)*

4 cups oil for frying

kosher salt

½ cup sliced chives for garnish

Italian parsley for garnish

TARTAR SAUCE

2 cups mayonnaise

⅓ cup cornichons, chopped

⅓ cup capers, drained

⅓ cup chopped red onion

juice of one lemon

kosher salt and pepper

Mix together the flour and cracker meal. Dredge the oysters in the flour mixture and shake off excess. Fry them in hot oil until golden brown. Drain on paper towels. Sprinkle lightly with kosher salt.

Mix together all tartar sauce ingredients. Spoon the tartar sauce into each shell and top with oyster. Arrange on a plate in a circle. Sprinkle with fresh chives and garnish with parsley.

Clams Casino

2 cups bread crumbs

¼ pound butter, melted

1 teaspoon paprika

dash of thyme

2 tablespoons parsley, chopped

salt and pepper to taste

24 clams

1 pound raw bacon

24 butter pats

Combine the first 6 ingredients and mix well. Shuck the clams. Cover them generously with the bread-crumb mixture. Cut the bacon in pieces to fit each clam. Use 1 piece of bacon and 1 butter pat per clam on the half shell. Bake or broil for approximately 8 minutes.

Eat Locally • Think Globally, Eat Locally • Think Globally, E
lly • Think Globally, Eat Locally •
t Locally • Think Globally, Eat Lo
k Globally, Eat Locally • Think G
Eat Locally • Think Globally, Eat
bally, Eat Locally • Think Globall
Globally, Eat Locally • Think Globa
Locally • Think Globally, Eat Loc
n, Eat Locally • Think Globally, E.
k Globally, Eat Locally • Think G
Eat Locally • Think Globally, Eat
bally, Eat Locally • Think Globall

And not a moment too soon. After twenty-four weeks of deliveries, of trying to keep things interesting and searching out novel vegetables, Thanksgiving is a holiday full of traditional foods that are pretty abundant around here in November. Some grub

THANKSGIVING: THE LAST DELIVERY OF THE SEASON!

seems to get eaten only on Thanksgiving. Quick, when was the last time you had a rutabaga? Or cooked a whole turkey, for that matter? Probably last Turkey Day. It is a holiday defined by certain dishes, more so than just about any other.

Oh sure, Passover has its Bread of Affliction, Christmas its cookies, Valentine's Day its chocolate hearts and licorice whips, but Thanksgiving is designed for eating. No bunnies with candy or large men in red flannel pajamas will be visiting your house (unless you're Hugh Hefner), and there's no candles, trees, or flags that you need to worry about. Just good food, family, tension, and football.

Thanksgiving is the farmiest of holidays. It's also the busiest farmers' market of the season. On the Wednesday before Thanksgiving, Union Square is jammed with customers, turnips, cabbages, big apples, good eggs, farmers, herbs, and us, trying to get ready for our biggest delivery of the season. The holiday seasons roll into one another, with the Christmas-tree farmers looking for those early, organized types who want their wreaths ready for Friday, and a few farmers now touting their unsold Halloween pumpkins as the perfect Thanksgiving centerpieces.

There's music at the market, too. The ubiquitous Peruvian pan flute players are there, selling their tapes and fluting for spare change. Manhattan is overrun with Peruvian pan fluters. I wonder if there's anyone left in Peru playing those darn things. Or is there some kind of vocational pan-flute education program there, churning out these fellows? It seems like every public space in New York has a group of Peruvian pan flute players in it. It can't be the same six guys;

there must be a flotilla of pan flautists in town. If it is all the same bunch, then they're making more money than the three tenors. People love that swinging pan flute sound. They always gather a good crowd of Yanni T-shirt wearing tourists. Pan fluters sound okay for a little while, but when they set up next to your farm stand for the day, well, there is a certain sameness to pan-flute music. It can drive you a little batty after a while. I hope there are hordes of American tuba players in Peru, setting up at open-air markets and playing Sousa marches.

And then there's "Black Elvis," who sits on a little chair at the market with his hat pulled low and plays the blues on his acoustic guitar. He's pretty good. He sounds a little like Richie Havens. Richie Havens is the guy who sang "Freedom" at Woodstock, but he's probably better known for his rendition of the "Cotton" theme song for TV commercials ("The touch, the feel, the fabric of our lives"). I asked Elvis to play the cotton song once; I even sang a few bars of it for him to get him started. He responded by playing his version of "Blowin' in the Wind" instead. I'm sure there was a message in that, but it was lost on me.

Besides the farmers and the musicians, there is another hard-working group looking to separate the customers from their money at the market, especially when it's this busy: pickpockets. "Caution: Pickpockets Are Working the Market!"

signs are hung up by the market managers at just about every farm stand, which I think adds a Dickensian flair to the market, especially in the cool of fall.

I have never actually seen a pickpocket there, but perhaps that's because when I scan the crowd for pickpockets, I am looking for Oliver and the Artful Dodger wearing grubby half gloves and a battered stovepipe hat. I guess the era of the charming pickpocket scalawag has passed, though, and New York must be short of Fagin types to pass along the trade.

We've been ripped off a couple of times—backpacks stolen from the cab of the truck; an occasional tomato is liberated—but my pocket has yet to be picked. (I starred in *Oliver* in fifth grade, a performance that still echoes through the halls of Dater School in Ramsey, New Jersey: "Please, Sir, I want some more.")

By all accounts, the farmers' market is a pretty safe place, though. Mohammed, the security officer there, is a mountain. The weight of his stare alone inspires good citizenship. And New York's Finest are always around, often buying some vegetables at the end of their shifts. My dad always gives them a discount. I think this is a holdover from the days when he owned a deli and always gave the cops free coffee.

At the market, we park our delivery van illegally at the edge of all the confusion. Much like construction workers with their orange traffic cones, I usually balance an onion crate on the hood or leave the back doors open, exposing our cargo of vegetables, identifying us as market insiders. So far, I have yet to get a ticket at Union Square, although I have gotten one just about everywhere else in town.

Just about every farmer has a bumper crop of pies at the Thanksgiving market. Apple, pumpkin, sweet potato, three berry, blueberry, cherry, mincemeat, quince, maple, and rhubarb are all piled high in pie pyramids, farmy and wholesome and looking for a good home. Every other hand, it seems, is outstretched, palm skyward, balancing some type of fruit-filled circle. For many of these pies, the journey is just beginning. They'll travel by subway to the Bronx, in a Range Rover to Connecticut, via overnight delivery to Grandma in Florida, or just saunter down the street to a loft in Soho.

My sister Cindy made a passel of pumpkin pies from scratch this year for our delivery customers and for Guy to sell at the market. Her house smelled like baking pumpkin guts for a few weeks afterward, and her hands turned that odd tanning-gel orange, but she did pretty well with them. I will be surprised, though, if pumpkin ever crosses her lips again. I never thought I would hear an innocent pumpkin cursed so thoroughly as I heard in Cindy's kitchen when Thanksgiving approached. Pumpkin had become the enemy; the awful orange orb.

The secret to a good pumpkin pie is to throw away your

can opener. Only fresh pumpkin should be used, preferably a sweet milk pumpkin, which you can get from a good grocery store or a farmers' market. It's pretty easy to make your own pumpkin goo, and it tastes a lot better. And if you're up to it, bake a lot of them and we'll sell them for you. I think there's an opening in our pie department.

I try to put together a nice holiday-theme delivery for our customers, but it can be tough. Some folks go out for dinner. Others have an army of guests over ("Ooh! Let's all gather around the organic sweet potato those nice delivery people brought us!"), and we couldn't possibly feed them all with one delivery package. Other people leave town and forget, in all the holiday hubbub, to tell us, returning to a bag of composting vegetables in their package room, their neighbors' dry cleaning smelling like funky lettuce. I try to stay away from the staple items, like mashed potatoes, and think of interesting side-dish possibilities.

This year, we included Brussels sprouts still on their stalks from David Yen's Hydro Gardens out on Long Island. Brussels sprouts are an odd-looking vegetable, like a green baseball bat with really bad warts and a head. I got six calls from people asking me what they were. (Don't they read the newsletter?!) "I had no idea they grew like that." One lady said that she thought that they grew in clusters on a vine, like grapes. People didn't recognize them without the little white supermarket box they're usually packed in. But that's okay. One of the rewarding things about this business is that in addition to providing good fresh food, I get to sneak a little learning into that delivery bag, too. And the sprouts were, after all, pretty funny-looking things. They're about four feet long and have a child-size noggin on top, which you can eat if you'd like. They look like nothing so much as little green men.

My recipe for Brussels sprouts makes a big impression. You'll hear a lot of "Gee, I don't usually care for Brussels sprouts, but these are delicious." Before you go patting yourself on the back, please know that you could substitute little superballs and it'd still be good. The sprouts are merely a vehicle for the bacon and blue cheese, which, in large enough amounts, will make most anything delicious.

Sometimes Brussels sprouts smell funny when you boil them, like a musty old sock. If you add a carrot to the water, the smell is diminished. I have no idea why this works, or what helpful-hints genius first figured it out ("Hey, this stinks—throw a carrot in it"), but it does seem to help. In fact, I put carrots in my sneakers at night occasionally, and although it doesn't diminish any aromas, it does give me a good chuckle when I look at them.

Brussels sprouts are also swell sautéed with walnuts in butter. Add a few drops of walnut oil at the end if you've got it. Boil the little darlings first for a few minutes. Add a little chopped fresh rosemary, some kosher salt, and some cracked pepper, and you're done. Maybe serve 'em on a bed of mesclun salad with a little goat cheese.

Now let's talk turkey. What is it with all the cauldrons of boiling oil? Perhaps in an effort to return the turkey to its place as the star of the meal, after years of being upstaged by side dishes, certain people have taken to deep-frying the holiday bird. Fried turkeys seem all the rage. They do taste pretty good, sort of the Colonel meets Miles Standish.

I guess a fried turkey is a fine thing if you've got an enormous pot you no longer want, and your clan breeds only well-behaved children who won't go near the potential catastrophe and who won't try to deep-fry the family pets. My brother sired three hellions who hit the ground running. A huge vat of hot fat is not part of our holiday traditions.

Bad deep-frying experiments are inevitable with that much hot oil around. "Gee, if it works on turkey, let's just fry the whole damn meal. No pots to wash!" And the oil always gets dumped in some corner of the yard, your own little Superfund site. No thanks. I'll stick with the tried-and-true turkey-preparation method. The one handed down from our founding fathers and mothers.

Barbecue.

What's more American than that? I doubt the pilgrims

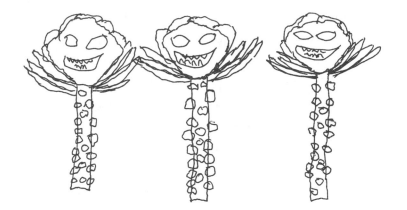

had a little plastic doohickey pop out of some prebasted bird to tell them it was time to eat. "Hey, Mrs. Pilgrim, is it done yet?" "Well, Miles, if you had gotten up early enough and put it in when I told you to, it would be done by now. But, no, instead here we are, with a cabin full of people, waiting for the doohickey to pop up. And turn off that damn lacrosse game or whatever it is, and come in here and give me a hand. They're your relatives, too, remember?"

They cooked over an open flame, which is perfect for Thanksgiving. A Turkey Day barbecue accomplishes many things. Folks like to hang out near a fire, so it gets people out of the house. Men, like moths, seem drawn to flame and often feel it their genetic duty to supervise any open-hearth cooking. Therefore, the menfolk will naturally feel responsible for the task of barbecuing the bird. This will free up space in front of the television, which, in turn, will help to keep the kids quiet. And should any little darlings venture outside, well, there will be a flock of men there to watch them. So a Thanksgiving barbecue quietly shifts two traditionally female roles to the male—cooking and kid tracking. It would seem like a conspiracy if it didn't taste so good.

Also, now the oven doesn't have a big bird in it taking up all the space. It seems to me that it's all the other stuff on the table at Thanksgiving that people really love. The stuffing, casseroles, mashed and creamed this and that, the pies, cookies, breads, chestnuts, all have to be made above, before, or around the bird in the oven. The turkey is just there to fuel the nap after the game. And yet everything must make way for the bird. A barbecued main dish is different and delicious, and an empty oven is a beautiful thing.

We usually have Thanksgiving at my sister Cindy and my brother-in-law Ray's house. Ray constructed the house out of an old barn, and it's roomy inside, which is one reason why we have our holiday there. We used to have it at my mom and dad's house in New Jersey, but my mother had gotten into the odd habit of inviting total strangers over for Thanksgiving dinner, unbeknownst to the rest of us. Usually it worked out fine, but there's enough confusion with just my family around and I hated the name tags. Anyway, Cindy's house is closer to the middle of nowhere, and the total strangers around there are too scary for my mom to ask over.

Alan Harding, chef and owner at Patois restaurant, in Brooklyn, New York, came to my brother's Turkey Harvest Party about six years ago and made a version of the recipe included. I stole it for Thanksgiving and it's been a hit ever since. It's important to use a fresh turkey (not frozen) and to marinate it. You might want to practice this once before the big day. Labor Day seems like a logical choice. The turkey can stand in for your boss.

Obviously, since the barbecued bird is split in half, it cannot be stuffed. I think this is just fine. Preparing food by steaming it inside an animal's body cavity has never been that appealing to me. This cornbread stuffing is made on top of the stove and is delicious.

MY SISTER CINDY'S
PIE OF THE PUMPKIN

All of the ingredients in this recipe are organic.

THE CRUST

1½ cups whole wheat flour

1½ cups white flour

1 tablespoon ground ginger*

1 teaspoon sea salt

1 teaspoon cinnamon

1 teaspoon maple sugar

1 teaspoon baking powder

¾ cup oil

¾ cup maple syrup

⅛ cup cider vinegar

THE FILLING

1½ cups pureed cheese pumpkin

1 teaspoon sea salt

⅔ cups maple sugar

1 teaspoon ground cinnamon

1 teaspoon ground ginger*

1 teaspoon vanilla extract

2 eggs, lightly beaten

½ cup light cream

For the crust: Preheat oven to 350 degrees. In a medium bowl, mix the flours, ginger, sea salt, cinnamon, maple sugar, and baking powder. In a large bowl, mix the oil, maple syrup, and vinegar. Add the dry ingredients to the wet and mix well. Roll crust out and press into a pie tin with your fingers. Bake for 30 minutes. Let cool.

For the filling: Preheat oven to 375 degrees. Combine all of the filling ingredients.** Pour into the cooled pie shell. Cover the rim with foil strips to prevent burning, and bake for about 1 hour.

*Measure ginger carefully, as too much leaves an aftertaste.
**Test the pumpkin mixture, as some pumpkins are so sweet that sugar is not necessary.

NICOLLE'S
PUMPKIN AND BASIL SOUP

1 medium to large pumpkin (milk
  pumpkins are the sweetest, but you
  can also use the good old jack o'
  lantern kind, too!)
olive oil
6 cups chicken stock
2 tablespoons butter

1 medium onion, chopped finely
1 medium to large tomato, chopped
  finely
2 tablespoons fresh basil, chopped
dash of real maple syrup
salt and pepper

Preheat oven to 350 degrees.

Carefully cut the pumpkin in half. Scoop out the seeds and strings. Rub the edges lightly with some olive oil, place on a cookie sheet, and bake for 30 to 40 minutes or until the pumpkin gets soft enough to remove the skin easily. Let it cool for a while, remove the skin, and chop coarsely.

In a medium to large soup pot, throw in the pumpkin with 5 cups of chicken stock. Set the remaining cup of stock aside to use later. Bring the pumpkin mixture to a boil and simmer over medium heat for about 20 minutes. Remove the mixture from the heat and puree in a blender or food processor. Return the pureed mixture to the soup pot.

In a medium saucepan, melt the butter. Sauté the onion

until soft and a little brown. Add the tomato and stew the mixture for 5 to 10 minutes. Remove from the heat and swirl the tomato and onion mixture into the pumpkin puree. If the soup is too thick, stir in the remaining chicken stock to thin, as needed. Stir in the chopped basil and a dribble of the maple syrup, and toss in some salt and pepper to taste.

Serve in warmed soup bowls with extra basil sprinkled on top for garnish. Complement with a warm crusty loaf of bread and a nice fruity glass of Beaujolais. Enjoy!

Root Vegetable Adobo

(cendrillon)

1 pound parsnips	1 pound sweet potatoes or yams
1 pound potatoes	dressing (recipe follows)

Preheat oven to 400 degrees.

Wash the root vegetables well. Quarter the parsnips lengthwise. Cut the potatoes into about ½-inch cubes. Toss the cut vegetables with dressing and pour into an oiled half-sheet pan. Roast for about 15 to 20 minutes.

Dressing

1 small bunch of basil, parsley, or cilantro, chopped	3 tablespoons olive oil or any vegetable oil
3 tablespoons miso	1 head of garlic, peeled and quartered
3 tablespoons mustard	
½ cup cider or rice vinegar	

Combine all ingredients in a large bowl.

DOUG'S GRILLED TURKEY

1 fresh turkey, about 18 pounds,
  split in half (the butcher will do it
  for you for free in about ten
  seconds)
3 bunches parsley, chopped fine
1 bunch rosemary, chopped

8 ounces good olive oil
10 garlic cloves, minced
juice of 5 lemons
salt and pepper
butter

Start the fire in the grill. You'll need a grill big enough to cook both halves at once. I use one of those big Weber kettles. Don't try this if your grill is too small. It'll take too long, your family will be hungry, and your wife will look at you funny. Charcoal is best, but gas will do.

Wash and dry the turkey.

Mix together all the ingredients except for the butter and, of course, the turkey.

Gently lift the skin of the turkey away from the meat in places and slip some of the olive oil–herb mixture in between. You might have to make little cuts in the skin to get the mixture everywhere you want it, but try not to take the skin off the bird. If you need more, well, just make some. Use a fairly good amount. Rub the turkey's skin with butter. Season liberally with salt and pepper. Wrap the seasoned bird in aluminum foil, the expensive, thick kind, 3 times. Marinate 1 hour at least. Place it on the grill, cut side down to start. Move it every half hour or so.

Cook about 3 hours, till the leg joint wiggles easily. Or you can use a meat thermometer, but you'll probably know when it's done because you've taken a taste.

Unwrap the bird and finish browning on the grill.

Remember to move the bird regularly, standing it on as many sides as is practical. This will require you to be outside in November, so remember to buy a little "cooking" brandy.

Also, as long as you've got the fire going, some nice grilled vegetables would be tasty. You can brush them with any of the leftover olive oil mixture you've got there, as long as you haven't contaminated it with any raw turkey. Let the bird rest a bit, then carve it up as usual, basking in how vigorous cooking outside in the cold can make you feel. (If you live where it doesn't get cold, use your imagination, and stop drinking all that brandy.)

CORNBREAD AND BOURBON STUFFING

(PATOIS)

THE CORNBREAD

1 small can of corn, drained	a little salt
2 cups cornmeal	1 egg
2 cups all-purpose flour	2 cups milk, room temperature
1 tablespoon baking powder	2 tablespoons vegetable oil

Sear the corn in a skillet with a little oil till the kernels are charred a bit on one side. Mix the dry stuff together. Add the seared corn kernels. Beat the egg. Add the milk and oil to that there egg. Pour the wet stuff into the dry stuff, and mix till just moist. Bake in a greased 8-inch-square pan at 375 degrees for about 20 minutes. Or go to the bakery and buy cornbread. Heck, just have the whole meal catered, why don't you? Either way, you'll have to cut the bread into 1-inch cubes and then let it sit for a couple of days, so plan ahead!

1 pound hot or sweet Italian sausage,
  the good kind

one glass of your favorite wine

3 apples, cut into chunks

½ cup pecan pieces or halves

2 onions, chopped

4 stalks of celery, leaves and all,
  chopped

4 tablespoons butter

6 ounces sweet heavy cream

¾ cup bourbon

1½ cups chicken broth, the low
  sodium kind

¼ cup fresh parsley, chopped

1 tablespoon fresh sage, chopped

Sauté the sausage in a big skillet. Remove meat and reserve juices.

Begin sipping one glass of your favorite wine.

Add apples and pecans to the same pan and sauté for 2 to 3 minutes. Remove. Add onion and celery and the butter. Sauté till golden and softened.

Add heavy cream to pan. Scrape loose any of the good stuff stuck to the bottom and stir for 1 minute or so. Don't burn the cream.

Add the meat, nuts, and apples back to pan. Mix it all up.

Warm the bourbon and chicken stock in a medium saucepan.

Mix the herbs and all of the cornbread cubes in a big bowl.

Add the onion-apple-sausage mixture and mix well.

Add the bourbon, chicken stock, and maybe a little of the juices from the sausage. You can either eat the stuffing right now or bake it for 25 to 30 minutes in the oven. Eat this only once or twice a year, or you'll kill yourself and your loved ones with it.

GRILLED ROSEMARY LAMB CHOPS

(THE GRANGE HALL)

Serves 6

1¼ cups olive oil

½ cup fresh rosemary, cleaned and
  chopped

2 teaspoons salt

½ tablespoon ground black pepper

12 pieces center cut loin lamb chops
  (1½ inches thick)

Combine the olive oil, rosemary, salt, and pepper. Coat both sides of the chops with the rosemary mixture and let marinate for at least 1 hour. On an open grill or broiler, cook the chops until the desired temperature is achieved—rare, medium, or well. Suggested ideal temperature is medium rare.

GOOD BRUSSELS SPROUTS

2 pounds or a bit more of Brussels
  sprouts
1 pound bacon
3 or 4 onions, chopped

¾ cup walnut pieces
1 tablespoon fresh rosemary
1 pound Stilton or Maytag blue
  cheese

Soak the sprouts in water for 5 minutes, then boil for 5 minutes. Cook the bacon in a big skillet till crispy. Drain the bacon and pour off the grease. Fry the onions in the same pan. Add the boiled sprouts to the pan. Add the walnuts to the pan. Sauté on medium to high heat till the sprouts get a bit browned in spots. Don't move them around too much. Sprinkle with rosemary. Cover with crumbled blue cheese. Broil till the cheese is bubbly and melted. Bask in the praise.

Vino de Brooklyn
by my mom

Ah! The euphoria!
In our Trat-tor-ia
Where the wine we have pressed is sublime.
The bouquet! Heady and sweet,
Francophiles can't compete!
Brooklyn's own "joie de vivre"
of the vine.

It's just about my favorite sandwich. Herbed potato croquets, deep-fried, with fresh creamy ricotta and salty Parmesan cheeses, and panelle, which is a sort of chick pea flour fritter, all on a warm, homemade sesame roll. It's a heart attack on a

MAKING WINE AT FERDINANDO'S FOCACCERIA

hard roll, I know, but it's delicious. I discovered this wondrous creation at Ferdinando's Focacceria. Sitting at one of the little marble tables with my newspaper, eating that fantastic sandwich, and watching all the people come in and out had become a favorite pastime of mine. I knew I had become a "regular" when the owner, Francesco Buffa, sat down across the table from me and struck up a conversation after the lunch rush. I felt like a comedian on Carson who'd been invited over to the couch after a good performance. Over the course of a few visits, we became friends. I'd bring him some extra basil or tomatoes from the deliveries, he'd give me a little espresso. We talked about food and restaurants, doing business in New York City, and farming.

Francesco's father grew lemons back in Sicily.

"How your brother do on the farm this year?" he asked me. His speech is accented by his Italian heritage. It's an easy rhythm to fall into, infectious, and during the course of our conversations, I occasionally find myself slipping into it, like a bad actor at a *Godfather* casting call.

"Not bad. Too hot, though, not enough a-rain. He had to a-water everything by a-hand," I replied, in my best inadvertent Brando.

"That's what a-my father used to do in Sicily. He used to use a route on the ground. All the water goes into one area, then you close that area, open another area. I remember for eight hours we used to do that. Sometimes at nighttime with flashlights."

"Were you on a hill?"

"No, no, it was a-flat. And you never know what time you going to get the water."

"It wasn't there all the time?"

"No, you gotta wait, sometimes for a month, you be on the list. Each property got the water one at a time. My father's property get the water for a-eight hours. The next property gets the water maybe twelve hours, in case maybe there's a little less. When I was a kid, I remember my father sometimes complaining to the people in town, 'Look, give me some a-water, all the plants, they're starting to get dry.' And they tell him, 'Listen, mister, we're busy in another area, maybe three or four days we come to your area.'"

"I don't understand. Did the water come by truck?"

"No, no, they had a well, and then they turn on the well, and they work for twenty-four hours a day. The water come along the ground in a canal. A little, like a little route, a stream. When they finish one area they move on. Sometimes they a-come to my father, they say, 'Listen, ten o'clock tonight, the water's coming. Tell your men.' You'd need some guys to change the route of the water. And you got to watch it the whole way. And turn it into a little section for the trees. A little section at a time. Open it, let the water in, and close it back up. And you only got maybe eight hours."

"That's a lot of work, huh?"

"Sure it is. Sometimes it wasn't ten o'clock, maybe it's one o'clock in the morning. Late, 'cause the water takes time to get to you. And you gotta watch it the whole way, make sure it gets to your farm."

"You have a big place?"

"Sure."

"Sicily is pretty dry?"

"Oh yeah, that's why the water's so important. We always wait for the water."

"What did you grow?"

"My father? He grow a lot of lemon trees. Orange tree. In the summer a little a-produce—lettuce, tomatoes. My father grow mostly the lemon, though. Say the water comes from over there. You close this area, open up this one, one at a time, thirty trees at a time. Sometimes the water would come from a-one mile away. The pressure's not very good. Sometimes everybody along the way, they take a little, just a little, but the pressure's not so good. We open up a little section, then close; we do that all night long to get the water to the lemons. Some figs, too, just for us, near the house."

So the water in Sicily came to the fields by way of a sluice. The amount of cooperation necessary for that to be successful would be hard to duplicate now.

"The fig tree here, behind the restaurant, it's from Italy?"

"This one here, it's from a-Italy, yes. We used to pick them near our house, so many figs. And sweet! Still warm from the sun. This one I got back here, it's good too, but not so much fruit."

Francesco offers me a ribbon of thick dark espresso in a little cup, sets down an old sugar pourer and a bottle with no label, half full of Sambuca. Ferdinando's Focacceria is in the Cobble Hill section of Brooklyn, cut off from the rest of this mainly Italian neighborhood by the Brooklyn Queens Expressway. It feels like a warp in time at Ferdinando's. It's small and cozy inside, casually romantic, populated mostly by regulars who come for the panelle, the pasta con sardi, and the delicious antipasto. A lot of the cooking is done right up front near the door, in an unusual setup, a sort of precursor to the open kitchen popular in a lot of tony restaurants today. There's another kitchen in the back that you have to walk through to get to the restroom, an arrangement that is common in New Orleans but rare in New York (and one that guarantees a clean kitchen). It was in this back kitchen where Francesco and I would make a little wine.

"In Sicily, most people made their own wine. Me, I haven't made it in about four years. I gave most of my tools to my friend, but we'll give it a try."

"I'd like to go to Sicily," I tell him. "Nicolle, she really wants to go there. Maybe we could visit a few farms over there, see how they do things. Oh, how's your basil back there in your yard, any better?"

"No, forget it. Disaster," he says, pulling on the first two syllables, "dee-saas-ter." "Every year the basil is very bad. Maybe some bird eats it, I don't know. I don't know what it is. Maybe too much water. My neighbor over there, he waters all the time and it runs down to my property. I can't stop it. In Sicily, tomatoes, the basil, they come a-beautiful! And we only water them once a month, maybe every two weeks. And they were so beautiful. The water's a little salty, there. Where I lived, it was a-two miles a-from the ocean. The well in the house, that water was a little salty, too. When you cut a tomato there, you don't need to put any salt or anything."

His backyard is tiny but full of life. Tomatoes grow underneath and next to two small fig trees.

"Here, you taste this," Francesco says, offering me a small dark fig. My fig experiences had previously been limited to the fig of Newton, but this fresh fruit exploded with sweetness. It was warm from the sun and perfectly ripe. He gave me about six of them, of two different varieties (which made me wonder if maybe he didn't really like the things so much himself). Between the two fig trees, a small statue of the Virgin Mary quietly watches over the little backyard.

In the front window of Ferdinando's Focacceria, Francesco had a wine press with an ivy plant in it.

"That thing work?" I asked him one day while devouring a stuffed artichoke.

"Sure," he said. "It works just fine."

"Well, you wanna make a little wine? I think I know a place to get some grapes."

A week later we were in his back kitchen, using an enormous old Mixmaster to knock the grapes off the stems. Grenache, they were, the color of a bruise, sweet and cold. I got them from a guy in the Bronx who trucks them in from California and sells them mainly to Italian-Americans and the occasional vegetable delivery boy.

"I don't know, they a little cold, these grapes," Francesco said. "It might take a few days for them to start to move, so we can press them."

"Move?" I asked.

"Yeah, you know, to move, to bubble up, to a-ferment," he explained, gesturing with his hands like he was tossing two balls into the air. "They got to a-warm up, maybe three, four days before we can press them. But it's okay, we'll see what happens. Use a-your hands there a little to squeeze the juice out of them."

After they were knocked off their stems with the Mixmaster (using the dough paddle, by the way), we poured them into an enormous pot. We rolled up our sleeves and plunged our hands into the cool grapes and squeezed the guts out of them. It was very squishy and satisfying.

I came back three days later. The grape press had been taken out of the window and put in the back kitchen.

"I don't know," Francesco said, "They not a-doing nothing. They not a-moving, yet. But it's okay. We'll see what happens."

Squeezing the grapes in the press was harder work than I had expected. And the kitchen was warm and steamy because Francesco was boiling a whole octopus for the seafood salad. It was an interesting scene. As the occassional bathroom user came by, I was on one side of the kitchen, red from exertion and purple from wiping my sweaty brow with my grapey forearm, and Francesco was on the other, in a halo of steam, pulling out the violet tentacle of an octopus to see if it was ready to eat yet. But since this was in Cobble Hill, folks were pretty used to making wine and boiling octopus.

"Gee, that's a tiny press you got there," one lady offered as she waited for a friend in the restroom. "My husband's is much bigger than that."

"Well, its a good thing you married him, Ma'am," I replied, experiencing a bout of press envy.

It took us six batches through the press to get most of the

juice out of the grapes. We got about eight gallons. Francesco left the last batch of fruit in the press all night, tightening it very slowly, and those grapes yielded the last, and the clearest, gallon of juice.

"A lot of this is going to be 'fetz,' garbage, that we'll have to leave behind in a-the bottle. But we'll get a-five or six gallons out of this. If it starts to move," he said.

"One time, I was a-making wine and I put it in my garage. Well, it got cold and stopped fermenting, so I bottled it. Then a couple of months later, I open it, and the bottle explode, just a-like champagne."

"So you made champagne by accident?" I asked him.

"No, not a-really," he said. "It's a-like a baby who comes out at six months instead of a-nine month. You got to put it in a incubator, you know, so she grows healthy, or something's missing. This wine, there was a-something missing."

We put our wine in Francesco's immaculate basement. It would be ready to drink in about sixty days, a brave little vintage. In a year's time it would be better, but we could try a little in a couple of months.

A week later he called me.

"Doug, this is Francesco from the restaurant. The wine, it's a-starting to move. I thought you would like to know." A little homemade wine, a potato sandwich, and maybe a little octopus salad. Fifty-nine days to go. La dolce vita.

Pepperonata alla Siciliana

(FERDINANDO'S FOCACCERIA)

green, red, and yellow bell peppers

nice Spanish onion (as many as you like)

olive oil

1 cup white vinegar, a little more if you're using a lot of peppers and onions

1 tablespoon sugar

1½ teaspoons salt

pepper

1 small jar capers

Gaeta or Sicilian olives

Seed the peppers, cut them into strips about as big as your finger, maybe a little bigger. Wash and pat dry. Slice the onion, not too thick, not too thin. Sauté the onion in olive oil till golden over low heat. Add peppers, cover, and cook 5 to 7 minutes over low heat. Add about a cup of vinegar. Sauté for 5 minutes more over very low heat, covered. Add a tablespoon or so of sugar, 1½ teaspoons of salt, and some fresh pepper, to make an "agrodolce" sauce. Remove from the heat. Stir in the capers and olives.

Serve cold.

WHITE BEANS WITH SAGE AND GARLIC

(COL LEGNO)

2 cups dry cannelini beans	*18 cloves*
¾ cup flour	*21 whole cloves of garlic*
2 large bunches of sage	*salt*
whole peppercorns	*olive oil*

Rinse and drain the beans. Toss with the flour. Cover with cold water and soak overnight. Put ⅓ of the beans in a glass container (a large jar will do; Col Legno uses a fishbowl). Layer with ⅓ each fresh sage and whole peppercorns, 5 cloves, 7 whole garlic cloves, salt, and a little olive oil. Repeat layers so you have 3 layers of beans and spices. Gently fill glass container with water. Leave a few inches empty at the top. Sprinkle the top with olive oil. Place the container in a large stock pot half full of water.

Simmer at a low temperature for 2 to 3 hours, until beans are al dente.

FIACCHERIA PASTA

(COL LEGNO)

2 to 3 cloves of garlic, minced

1 red onion chopped

olive oil

1 16-ounce can of Italian plum
  tomatoes

6 ounces pancetta, cubed

salt and pepper

1½ tablespoons crushed red pepper

Sauté garlic and onion in a little olive oil. Add the tomatoes. Cover and simmer for 20 minutes.

In another pan, sauté cubed pancetta on low for about 10 minutes. Drain the pancetta. Add to the tomato sauce. Add a little salt and pepper. Add crushed red pepper.

Serve over spaghetti with fresh Romano cheese.

POACHED TROUT IN ALMOND MILK WITH GREEN BEANS AND VERMICELLI NOODLES

(VERBENA)

Serves 4

6 tablespoons butter	4 10-ounce whole brook trout
3 carrots, diced	1 cup vermicelli glass noodles
3 celery stalks, diced	½ pound green beans, blanched
1½ onions, diced	salt and pepper
1½ fennel bulbs, diced	3 cloves
1 bunch each of fresh tarragon and	1 teaspoon nutmeg
parsley leaves	2 cups court bouillon or chicken
¾ cup toasted almonds	stock
4 cups milk	
3 cups water	

In a 2-quart saucepan, melt 4 tablespoons of butter and add the vegetables. Cook until softened, about 15 minutes. Do not color.

Add the herbs, toasted almonds, milk, and water. Simmer until desired flavor is reached, about 20 minutes. Strain off and reserve the liquid. Reserve 1½ cups of the vegetables. Process the remaining vegetables in a food processor, and use ½ cup or so of the puree to thicken the sauce.

Place the whole trout in a large casserole. Pour half of the almond milk over the fish. Cover with a lid and poach at medium heat until cooked through, about 7 minutes. Put the chicken stock into a saucepan to finish the sauce. Add the pureed vegetables, glass noodles, and remaining butter. Before serving, add the blanched green beans. Transfer the fish to a plate and stuff the cavity with the reserved vegetables.

Pour glass noodles and sauce onto a serving dish. Place fish on top of noodles and sauce. Garnish with toasted almonds.

Local Fish Roasted with Herbs and Seasonal Vegetables

(JUDSON GRILL)

Serves 8

8 sprigs each of fresh rosemary,
  thyme, and parsley
6 tablespoons extra virgin olive oil
48 ounces fish fillets, left whole or
  cut into 8 6-ounce pieces
salt and pepper

2 lemons, halved
2 tablespoons parsley, chopped
2 tablespoons chives, chopped
Seasonal Vegetables (recipe
  follows)

Preheat oven to 500 degrees.

Place the herb sprigs and 2 tablespoons of olive oil in a large nonstick sauté pan. Season the fish with salt and pepper, and place on top of the herbs. Roast for 5 to 8 minutes, depending on fish thickness and desired doneness. When the fish is done, remove it carefully from the pan. Pull off the herbs. Squeeze the lemons over the fish. Drizzle with the remaining oil and the chopped herbs. Serve on top of the vegetables.

2 heads of garlic, split	*4 tablespoons extra virgin olive oil*
1½ pounds squash, beans, or other	*4 ounces water or vegetable stock*
seasonal vegetable	*salt and pepper*

Preheat oven to 400 degrees.

Roast the garlic heads for 30 minutes, until soft. Remove and let cool. When cool, squeeze out the garlic. Reserve.

For the vegetables:

- if using zucchini, slice thick
- if using wax beans, clean and blanch al dente
- if using broccoli, cut into small florets and blanch al dente
- if using carrots or other root vegetables, clean and cut into small pieces; blanch al dente

Add the garlic and oil to a pan over high heat. When the garlic starts to sizzle, add the vegetables and lightly brown. Add the water or stock and season with salt and pepper.

Eat Locally • Think Globally, E
lly • Think Globally, Eat Locally •
t Locally • Think Globally, Eat Lo
k Globally, Eat Locally • Think G
Eat Locally • Think Globally, Eat
obally, Eat Locally • Think Globall
Globally, Eat Locally • Think Globa
Locally • Think Globally, Eat Loc
y, Eat Locally • Think Globally, E
k Globally, Eat Locally • Think G
Eat Locally • Think Globally, Eat
bally, Eat Locally • Think Globall

THE SUBURBAN INVASION
BY MY MOM

The deer are here!
Here! Are the deer!
But not in the forest primeval.
They're chomping and chewing
the greens of the 'burbs
and causing a bit of
upheaval.
Not! Over the hills and far away,
out where the eagles soar,
But meandering hungrily out
of the woods,
Knocking at our front doors.
They know! They are handsome,
some pretty, some cute,
these very professional looters.
And though they may nibble
each seedling we've sown,
They're sure we won't reach
for our Shooters.
Yes, the deer are here,
Here are the deer!
Not roaming the land of the free.
So fence in the garden,
stand guard at the pass,
(and the deer have requested TV!).

Around 17,000 deer were killed by bowhunters in New Jersey last year. Over 10,000 were killed in collisions with motor vehicles. Which means that you have almost as good a chance of bagging a deer by just driving around as you do by actually trying to shoot one

DEER HUNTING IN SUBURBIA

with a bow and arrow. Suburban New Jersey is a tough place to be a deer. The woods are disappearing, the streets are choked with cars, and the few habitats remaining are crawling with hunters. Bowhunters, hunters with shotguns, rifles, and muzzle loaders are all out there, waiting to nail Bambi.

During hunting season, a walk in the woods can be a life-threatening excursion for a deer. And it's not much safer for a person. We sell a lot of leaves, grasses, and berries at the farmers' market beginning in the fall, and all that stuff has to be gathered out in the woods. So we avoid fawn-colored clothes, don our blaze orange, and enter the battlefield. We make a lot of noise, so we don't sneak up on any heavily armed, bleary-eyed hunters sitting in tree stands, and we probably scare away some of their prey.

Singing "I am not a deer, ain't no deer near here" while traipsing noisily through the woods picking rose hips and maple leaves may not endear me to any nearby hunters, but it's better than an arrow through my flank.

On a Saturday afternoon during hunting season, deer can be seen strapped to the backs of sedans, flopped into the beds of pickup trucks, or placed neatly in drop cloths and carried in minivans, behind the child seat, where the groceries usually go. The report of shotguns and rifles is frequent. A "pop" followed quickly by another shot usually means a miss, or a nonlethal hit. That hunter will be spending the late evening following the blood trail of the deer through the woods.

The bowhunters say that their method is more humane, that it's a more natural way of hunting, but either way, it's a bit grisly, all those deer carted down the highway with their tongues lolling about.

And yet the white-tailed deer is thriving in the area, as common as the squirrel in parts, and becoming a serious nuisance to farmers throughout the Northeast. At my brother's farm, about twenty-five miles north of the Jersey state line, the deer could decimate an entire season's worth of pumpkins, lettuces, and herbs in a single evening, and often they selectively chew only the most tender parts of a plant. Like most farmers, Guy has a permit to shoot them out of season, but it's impossible to shoot them all. It's kind of depressing, too. Deer are pretty cute critters, after all.

But cute or not, all those Bambis were eating a fortune in baby lettuces, so Guy put up an eight-foot-high wire fence around the whole place to keep them out, creating a sort of vegetable gulag. The deer still managed to break in at times, though. They would jump over the fence where it ran below a hill. They'd sneak under it where it crossed a stream. And, once those two venues were blocked, they began to saunter down the driveway at night. All those tender veggies planted neatly in rows for them were just too hard to resist. Sometimes they wouldn't plan their escape very well and they'd forget how they got in. That generally was not a mistake that they got to repeat.

I know that a lot of people are against hunting, and I've never been a real big hunter myself. I just couldn't pull the trigger. In fact, I caught a fish once at the Jersey shore, and I felt so bad about the hole the hook had left in its mouth that I wanted to take it to the vet before I threw it back.

But hunting does serve a purpose, I suppose, even if I'll never be much of a participant. There are too many deer in this area. They damage what few farms are left, and they do get whacked by cars a lot.

And, darn it, they taste good, especially those pumpkin- , herb- , and baby-lettuce-fed ones up on the farm. If I'm not opposed to eating them, I can't really be opposed to hunting them. That's life at the top of the food chain, I guess.

My friend Eddie Jarvis is the only guy I know well who hunts regularly. His hunting ground is suburban New Jersey, right near where we grew up. Eddie and I have been friends since we were little kids, so I can ask him as many dumb questions about hunting as I want, and he has to answer them.

For our first hunting excursion, I had planned to wear antlers and a red Rudolph nose, but I couldn't find any that fit. I also brought a whistle along with me, should a sudden pang of conscience hit me as a deer approached. "Run! Run for your lives, little deer!" I imagined I would yell, blowing my whistle and waving my arms wildly. (This behavior would probably just succeed in getting the deer to hold still while they looked quizzically at the crazy human, allowing Eddie to get off a clean shot.)

Most of the men in Ed's family hunt, and it was passed on to him. (My family goes to the supermarket meat department, which is also hereditary.) The hunting trip I tagged along on took place on an afternoon in mid-October.

"This time of year, this is the middle of the rut," Eddie says. "You know what the rut is?"

"Nope. What's the rut?" I ask. "I've been in a rut," I offer.

"This is a little bit different, Doug. There's a pre-rut, there's a rut, and a post-rut."

Sounds pretty similar to the rut I knew of so far. This conversation is taking place in Eddie's car, as we drive through Ramsey, New Jersey, where we grew up. This is not the country. There's a great deal of traffic around here, and most of the deer in town can be found at Blockbuster video.

We stop at a drugstore so I could buy film to chronicle our excursion.

I get back in the car, and Eddie continues explaining the rut.

"The pre-rut is in the beginning of fall. That's when the bucks mark their territory with rubs and scrapes," he says. "During the actual rut, when the does are in heat, all the buck thinks about is mating. That's when they get stupid and forget most of the instincts that keep them alive. They're not as attuned to what's going on around them. They're just concentrating on finding the female deer."

"Imagine that," I say.

"So that's what we're hoping for now—oh, shoot, I forgot my call. We have to go back to the house."

"A deer call?"

"Yeah. It's called a grunt."

"So you just grunt at them, and they find this attractive?" I ask.

"Yup. It makes a grunting noise. You can also get two antlers and click them together. It helps to lure them in. But the best opportunity is knowing the land that you're hunting. And staying upwind of your prey.

"Mostly, deer depend on their sense of smell and their hearing," Eddie continues. "If a deer hears something, they may prick their ears up, but if they don't smell anything, they'll just go back to what they were doing. But once a deer winds you, gets that scent, it'll just bolt.

"When you're hunting and you hear the leaves rustle, it could be a mouse, it could be a squirrel, you get this rush of adrenaline," he says. "And then when you're about to shoot a deer, or you're watching someone else about to shoot one, like when my cousin gets one, it feels like your heart is going to jump right out of your chest. That's what they call buck fever," he explains.

"And you don't feel bad about killing the poor little critter?" I ask.

"No, I don't for a few reasons. One, it's better for you than what you get in the supermarket. It's healthier. I only believe in killing what you're going to take in and use. If I didn't like venison, then I wouldn't kill a deer. Also, especially around here, where there used to be more woods and now it's more of a suburban type of place, they're getting killed walking across the street, and they're starving in the wintertime."

"How many deer are you allowed to take?" I ask.

"They used to be more strict. Fish and Game, they actually want you to kill more does now, for population control."

We are stuck in traffic on our way through town to Eddie's hunting grounds, which are less than five miles from his house. It's a property along the Ramapo River where a friend of his owns a house and a few acres of woods.

Hunting in New Jersey is often done in the nooks and crannies forgotten by development. Hunters, like the deer they're after, have had to adapt as suburban open space becomes rarer. In central Jersey, I've seen people hunting behind a Kmart. You could park your car in the lot, go into the store, buy some camouflage gear, put it on, grab your gun, walk behind the store, and start hunting.

Increasingly, there's been a problem with guys actually hunting from their cars along the sides of the road, so the Fish and Game Department put out a decoy deer along a highway and arrested the hunters who shot it.

"It's been pretty successful," says Captain Glen Hawkswell, of the New Jersey Fish and Game Law Enforcement Division. "We've also used decoy pheasants and turkeys. One guy even got what we call a Grand Slam. He's been arrested for shooting at all three types of our decoys from a car. The penalties are pretty minor," he says, "fines between two hundred and one thousand dollars, but it's so embarrassing to get caught that it's been a pretty good deterrent."

The traffic clears and we make our way up Darlington Avenue to where we'll be hunting. The land is owned by a retired doctor who raises Brittany hunting dogs and quail. It's a nice spot, backing up to the river, one of a short string of beautiful estates along the Ramapo. It is incredible to me that a place like this exists here. The rest of the area is so built up. But this is like a secret nature preserve, and it backs up to a county park. I've seen deer along the road here and in people's backyards as well.

"Deer have a sense of where they're safe and where they're not," Eddie says. "That's why I think we might get lucky here. No one else is hunting on this property."

"You didn't get one last year did you?" I ask him.

"No. I like getting them, don't get me wrong. But I don't mind if I don't sometimes, though. I just like being out in the woods. You're dressed in camo and you're quiet. It's like you're more part of the natural surroundings. I've seen big owls, coyotes go running by, bears."

We pull into the long driveway and the dogs start barking. Beautiful Brittanys, red and white, barking and jumping behind an electronic fence. The house is big, pretty new, and looks expensive. This property must be worth around a million dollars, and I feel a little like Robin Hood poaching in Sherwood Forest.

I slip Eddie's spare camouflage jumpsuit over my jeans and T-shirt, and my entire personality changes. The macho that is in every man comes out. I look ridiculous with my bright red gloves, the little snack I've packed, my camera, and my camos on, but I don't care. I am a hunter. Suddenly, I don't need my whistle any longer; I won't be sparing any deer. I need a bow and arrow of my own. Or a shotgun, a slingshot, a spear, something, something to kill with. Camo gear! I'm wearing a camouflage jumpsuit, and I am a hunter, out in the wilderness. It matters not that I'm less than two minutes from the closest McDonald's, I've got to go out into the woods and bring down some meat!

Ed pulls his macho bow out of the macho trunk of his macho Honda. This is not Robin Hood's bow. It looks very silent and lethal. The arrows have razors on their tips. It is a compound bow with pulleys and some kind of trigger mechanism on it.

The fellow who owns the place drives up on an all-terrain vehicle. He is friendly and pleasant, telling us about his dogs and the birds that he raises here. Eddie thanks him for letting us hunt on his property.

"Oh no problem," he says. "In fact, shoot them all. You can't stop them. The dogs keep them away from the house, but they're all over the place out here."

We enter the woods. Eddie points out places on the trees where the bucks have rubbed off the bark with their antlers to mark their turf.

"I think they'll be coming off that hill in the evening, so we'll set up over there," he says.

He is carrying some type of tree stand contraption on his back. It looks heavy and cumbersome, but he handles it easily.

We hear them before we see them. A rustling on the hillside just ahead of us, just a few minutes after we enter the woods. I immediately think that it's a deer, but Ed isn't so sure. Then, along the ridgeline about sixty yards away, we see a large flock of wild turkeys through the trees. They see us too and hightail it out of there, running swiftly through the woods. My heart is pounding, and I realize that it's a good thing I don't have a weapon, because I would've just shot a tree.

Eddie picks out a suitable spot and loops part of the tree stand around the trunk of an oak and the other part around his feet. Somehow, this device allows him to sort of walk up the side of the tree using a kind of back and forth rocking motion, while his weapon trails below him on a rope. It is really an ingenious device, and I am jealous that I'll just be sitting on the cold ground with my camera and my snack. My blood lust has subsided and I'm leaning more to the deer's side of the equation again. It's the first time I've seen Ed climb a tree since we were little kids at one of my backyard birthday parties.

I brush the crunchy leaves away from the base of a nearby tree and plop down onto the ground about ten yards away.

"Hey, Ed, what if the deer comes right over here where I am?"

"Duck," he replies.

After sitting still in the woods for a little while, I can feel my senses sharpen. My hearing, especially, seems to be keener. The noises I hear are a perfect suburban mixture of country and city sounds. A kid playing somewhere, pretty far off. Dogs barking. And quite a few airplanes overhead. A light breeze is blowing, and I can hear the leaves as they drop to the ground, like the crunch of a piece of toast. (I haven't had my snack yet.) Crows are calling to each other. And a blue jay squawks, such a beautiful bird with such a lousy voice. I can hear a dump truck backing up at a nearby construction site, and the sound of traffic out on Route 202 is almost constant. But it's pretty quiet in here; the pen scratching across the paper I'm taking notes on is noticeably audible.

It's getting later. We've been here for almost two hours with no sign of any deer. But Eddie's right; it is nice to just sit in the woods and look and listen. The only time I'm in the woods lately is when I'm looking for my golf ball, and I've never just sat perfectly still any place for two hours. It's hard for me to sit still at a movie, let alone under a tree. There's a lot going on in the woods, though. And unlike when I'm hiking or collecting cuttings to sell at the farmers' market, being still in the woods does give you a chance to become more a part of your environment. (Have you read my other book, *Walden?*)

Eddie signals to me from his place on high. He points at his wrist. "What time is it?" he mouths.

"Four, five, oh," I mouth, holding up four, then five fingers, followed by a fist. I feel like a Marine in my camo gear signaling like that. I know that he really wants to get a deer while I'm here with him for the book, but I am enjoying myself quite a bit. (Although a chapter entitled "Two Guys in Camouflage Sitting in the Woods with a Weapon" probably would've been cut.)

The birds are getting louder as the sun goes down. We hear a hawk cry overhead and then the bleat of some small critter that was probably its dinner. The slanting sun is directly in my face, warm and bright. It illuminates the silk of a spider's web between Eddie and me. I am admiring the spider's handiwork when I hear something big rustling in the leaves about forty yards away, directly behind Eddie. It's much louder than anything else I've heard—the turkeys, the squirrels, the wind. It even sounds louder to me than Eddie and I did, making our way to this spot.

"Ed!" I stage whisper. "Behind you ! A deer! A big one!" I mouth the words as loud as I can. But he has heard the rustling, too, and stands up slowly in his tree stand. He quietly picks up his bow, adjusting the trigger thing he wears on his hand. I can see the animal's coat clearly through the trees now, although I can't make out its head or tail. It is dark colored, almost black, with a bright pink blaze across its midsection. I have a perfect shot, but I have no weapon. I look up at Eddie, who has sat back down on his perch, smiling. The deer moves laterally. It is huge.

It is a horse. With a pink-sweatshirt-clad rider. And I am glad once again that Ed is doing the trigger pulling.

We never did see a deer in those woods. But it was a nice experience, nevertheless.

As we pull out of the driveway onto Route 202, a buck with a nice set of antlers runs across the road directly in front of us. If we had left five seconds earlier, we would've hit it head on. From the other side of the road, his eyes shine in the headlights as he stands and watches us drive away.

VENISON LOIN WITH SAGE AND ALLSPICE

(SAVOY)

1 2½- to 3-pound loin of venison,
   trimmed of fat
½ cup parsley leaves
1 cup sage leaves
¼ cup ground allspice

2 tablespoons Dijon mustard
6 cloves garlic, sliced thinly
2 teaspoons salt
¼ cup olive oil

Preheat oven to 400 degrees.

Cut the cleaned venison loin into equal parts. Set aside.

Make a spice paste: Combine the parsley, sage, and allspice in a food processor and process until well combined. Add everything else but the oil and process until smooth, then add the oil. Rub the venison with the paste, giving each piece a thin coating. Save the remaining paste for future use.

Heat a large skillet with 2 ounces of olive oil until smoking. Sear the venison on all sides and place in the skillet in the oven. Roast for 10 minutes for medium rare, longer for more well-done temperatures. Remove from pan and let rest 1 minute before slicing.

EDDIE'S
VENISON STEW

2 cups chicken broth

2 pounds venison meat, cubed

3 onions, diced

2 whole garlic cloves

1½ cups carrots, chopped

2 large baking potatoes, cubed

red wine

½ cup chopped fresh basil

salt and pepper

Bring the chicken broth to a boil. Add the venison and reduce to a simmer. Cook on low heat for 1 hour. Add carrots, potatoes, and a splash or two of wine. Simmer for another hour. Add basil, salt, and pepper. Cook for 30 minutes. (If you like a thicker stew, add a flour and butter roux at this point.)

Serve over egg noodles or sausage bread. Oooh, that's good!

There's nothing on Route 208 to indicate that it is there. No sign, nothing visible from the road. Which is probably how my brother prefers it. Just the end of a shale driveway blending into a dangerous curve on the busy street. After going through the small parking area at the top of

MY BROTHER'S FARM

the hill, where the far workers park their battered cars (and where I once stacked spools of copper wire), the plantings start. Herbs and flowers on both sides of the driveway. Cosmos, some grapevines, gnarled rosemary plants that look like bonsais from years of clipping them, a small plastic greenhouse on the right side that Guy grows Sungold tomatoes in to get a jump on the season. Feverfew and chamomile grow next to a couple of short rows of Saint-John's-wort, which I suggested Guy plant. It hasn't grown much this year; it's only a few inches tall and it never flowered. Maybe it's depressed, I don't know.

My brother's house is on the left side of the driveway, surrounded by a picket fence. It must be starting to feel a little bit smaller now that his three sons are starting to get so big. The barn is at the bottom of the hill, next to a stream that my brother uses to pump water out of for irrigating.

Across the driveway, on the right side of the barn, sit five old rusting trucks parked neatly in a row. It's a law of some sort in upstate New York that all agricultural property over two acres must have at least one rusting hulk on it, preferably on cinderblocks. Guy has two ancient hay trucks with wooden rack bodies, an old dump truck full of returnable bottles, and a groovy-looking canary yellow 1957 pickup truck that we used to go to the farmers' market in, before it got too scary to drive. Somehow, the old trucks add something to the place, and Guy seems reluctant to get rid of them. In fact, he once sent away the tow truck that had come for an old station wagon because he and the boys hadn't had their farewell party for it yet.

In front of the barn, there's a patch of strawberries, just for eating, not for selling, and a few rows of sunflowers. Next to the house is a little root cellar full of potatoes, garlic, and mason jars for canning.

Most of the farm is located on the other side of the stream. Three plastic greenhouses of descending height are used for storage, for growing stuff, and for making wreaths during the holidays. The fields around the greenhouses are where all the lettuces and other greens are planted. Red mustard, purple kale, green romaine, and lots of other varieties that go into Guy's mesclun salad grow in long straight rows.

The weeds, too, seem to grow in rows, taking up most of the space that isn't under cultivation (and taking up some of the cultivated ground, too). Because Guy grows everything organically, he doesn't use any herbicide on the weeds, just a hoe and hard work. Out back behind the lettuce fields, Guy grows his heirloom tomatoes, squash, corn, and other vegetables. More flowers grow on the right side of the field, near the stream, and Guy has wheat planted up on the hill to the left, behind his neighbor Joe Dolson's place.

Farther out back is the summer kitchen, the hammock, and the horse pasture, where my brother's two old horses, Shandilee and Prezwalski, live out their retirement. All in all, it's a nice little setup, comfortable and well worn.

Part swamp and pretty rocky, it's not really classic farmland, which makes it even more remarkable that my brother is able to coax such beautiful produce out of his farm.

As I've mentioned, the people who work with my brother at the farm are mainly from Mexico. Most of them have been with Guy for a long time. Rosa and Ramiro have been working with Guy for almost ten years. Rosa makes most of the flower arrangements for the market, and Ramiro is sort of Guy's foreman.

My sister Cindy has been doing most of the markets in the city for Guy, along with Guy's friend Nadine and my dad. The customers at the stand like to talk to my dad (especially the ladies), and he's got his own cast of "regulars" that will buy only from him. My sister has a habit of giving her favorite people a little discount, especially those that seem shy or quiet. "I always give that man a discount on his flowers," she told me once, after a debonair-looking gentleman left carrying two bunches of cosmos. "He might not have a lot of money, but he always buys his flowers, every week."

"Cindy," I told her, "that's Geoffrey Beene; he's a famous clothing designer. He has more money in the toe of his shoe than we make in a year." I think my sister has given his cosmo discount to somebody else now. Probably Ralph Lauren.

I go to the market a couple of times a week to see what's coming available for our deliveries, to talk to the farmers, or to help out at the stand. Usually, though, I'm there to get ready for a delivery.

After seeing what's available from my brother, I call

David Yen out on Long Island first. I like the quality of his produce, and he is very organized. He knows that we need everything to be packaged individually, so when I tell him that I need 120 pounds of green beans, he knows that I mean 120 one-pound units of beans, not just a single big bag of them. This makes my job a lot easier.

I have four phone numbers for David—home, office, barn, and cellular—and I still always get his answering machine. When he calls me back, it's usually the same routine. Even if it's our third conversation of the day, he always starts off the same way:

"Hello, Doug Jones, I'm David Yen," he announces in his Chinese accent, like we've never met. I always get a kick out of that, him using our full names, as though he's concerned that I might get him mixed up with all the other Chinese guys named David who are returning my phone calls. I guess that's how they do things where he's from. His English is just fine, though, much better than my Chinese. And he's always helpful, especially during those times of the year when good produce is hard to find. The growing season is a little longer on Long Island, and David has a lot of greenhouses as well. They help to stretch his season even more.

Once a year or so, we put together a package of all Asian produce, a "theme bag," and for a week we change our name to "My Chinese Brother." David writes that as the title of the newsletter in Chinese for me across the top of our letterhead. (At least that's what he says he's writing; I really have no way of knowing.) We include a lot of interesting vegetables, all ridiculously good for you, and recipes on how to cook them, along with some Asian marinade made by David's wife, Julie, which will be the "Tasty Morsel" for the week. David is very dependable and he always shows up, even when the weather is lousy. More than once, he's come to market just to deliver to me and then return home, five hours round-trip.

After speaking to David, I'll call one of the other farmers who we buy from regularly. Ken Migliorelli is one. He has one of the biggest stands in the market, with a good variety at a good price. I like to get beets from him, as well as little watermelons and broccoli rabe. Like a lot of the other farmers who come to market, the land around his farm is increasingly being built up. This is nothing new to the Migliorellis, though. They used to farm in the Bronx not that long ago.

"The pressure on the land is always increasing," he said over lunch at the Heartland Brewery. "No one is ripping out houses or condominiums to put in more farms." Which is true. No one is. They're just naming the new developments after the farms they are replacing.

The Smiths, Sue and Henry, at Sycamore Farms, are a good source for delicious sweet corn. Their claim to farmers'

MY BROTHER'S FARM
ORGANIC PRODUCE AND
TASTY MORSELS
212·615·6733
SUPPORT your local FARMER!

market fame is their "same-day corn." A second truck arrives
at the market later in the morning with corn picked that day,
so fresh it's still growing. The corn is so sweet you don't even
have to cook it, and the price is good.

At the market on Wednesday mornings, we go around to
each farm stand, gather up our orders, and pack them in the

van. We make up each bag as we arrive at our customer's location, and deliver it, usually to the doorman of the apartment building.

On the New York City food chain, one of the few creatures that a doorman doesn't have to take orders from is a delivery person, and sometimes they like to hassle us. Edicts such as "Go to the service entrance" or "You have to take it up yourself, you can't just leave it here" could add hours to our route by the end of the day. Mostly, it's no big deal and they're happy to accept delivery, especially after they see that we're coming back every week. Sometimes I'll give them some strawberries or a melon, and occasionally they'll request something specific from the market. Once, on East Forty-ninth Street, I realized when I got back to the van that I had forgotten to give our client the newsletter, so I ran back with it. When I got there, the doorman was shoving the blueberries from our bag into his mouth, his lips all covered with blue juice. He was so shocked to see me and he was very embarrassed. We replaced the berries. The next week I brought him his very own pint of strawberries. I never told the client, and I guess the doorman never did either. I wonder, though, how much stuff he had been eating all season long.

On Central Park West, one of the nicest streets in town, a doorman once took the bag of veggies and flung it out into the road, the spaghetti squash rolling unharmed across the busy street, and apples flying into the side of a passing taxi. I guess he was upset that we didn't use the service entrance. Or maybe he had had a bad experience with produce once, I don't know. We never saw him again. And the doormen in that building were always really nice to us from then on. The client was a Supreme Court judge.

Ninety-nine percent of the time, though, the doormen are great, and they seem to like chatting with our delivery people (who happen mainly to be attractive young women). We depend on the doormen, and they're generally very reliable. I think that they make pretty decent money, although being a doorman seems to be a hard job to stay focused in for very long. But I suppose that's all relative. Many of the doormen seem to be immigrants from Slavic countries. Given what's been happening in that area of the world of late, the opportunity to come to New York and make a decent living holding open a door and accepting packages without anyone trying to shoot you must seem pretty great. Back when I was a Corporate American, I don't recall envying guys who drove a delivery van around all day, but now I think it's wonderful.

My brother's mesclun is in the delivery just about every week. Most of the restaurants that have recipes in this book buy Guy's mesclun. It's his lettuces and his heirloom tomatoes that he is best known for. That and his personality. "Hey, guys, I sold something! Did you? Did you sell anything yet?"

he'll shout to the other farmers when he works the market if it's been a little slow. It's when he's packing up to go home that he really gets going. "Hey, hey, hey, it's the organic happy hour now, it's all half price now," Guy's voice booms across the market on late summer afternoons. "It's between you and the chickens, half price! Organic happy hour! Don't panic, its all organic!"

Business at the market seems to have fallen off a bit over the past few years, but Guy has managed to make up the difference by increasing his wholesale business to the restaurants. And My Brother's Farm has become one of my brother's farm's biggest customers.

I'd like to get another place, to grow stuff just for the deliveries. But I'm not so sure that I could give up living in the city entirely. I'd miss all the stimulation, the great restaurants, the constant parade that is New York. There's a lot of country life even here, and people seem to be more interested in finding a connection to the Earth more of late. Our little business does help to support local farms in a small way, and we have fun doing it, most of the time. Plus, that farming looks like mighty hard work. For now, I'll just keep schlepping those veggies around this ridiculous, wonderful city, maybe plant a flower or two, set loose a few bugs, and eat some oysters. If you're in town, come on by the farmers' market. And wear your old clothes.

NOVEMBER 21

The frost is on the pumpkin, the hay is in the barn, the oak
leaves have all gone russet, the russets are all in the root cellar,
there's thin ice on the pond each morning. (Actually, we don't
really have a pond, but I liked the imagery.) We're saddling up
our Old Paint, making a list and checking it twice, going over
the river and through the woods (to the cliché machine) one last
time for 1998, and gee, have you ever, what a real swell party it's
been. Thanksgiving marks our final delivery for the year, since
we are committed to bringing you 100 percent local produce,
and there's only so many times we can give you root vegetables
without eventually being stoned by rutabagas. All in all, it's
been a swell year. We've had a lot of fun running this tiny cor-
poration, and we're looking forward to next spring (when we're
being bought by Microsoft). Lots of you have taken us up on our
offer to sign up now for next season. Thanks a lot. (You like us!
You really like us!) Well, we think you're pretty great, too. In
our own small way, we've all helped local farmers. Hopefully,
we've eaten a bit healthier, too, expanded our palates a little, and

gotten more use out of all those pots and pans in our kitchens. Of course, now our vegetable standards have all been raised some. "You call that lettuce? That's not lettuce! I'll tell you what lettuce is!" And from what I've heard, we've got a few newly coined gourmets, too. "Yo! Chef guy! Move over! You're mucking it all up! Just sauté it in a little olive oil and garlic!" (The My Brother's Farm Official Default Recipe) Mostly, what I've learned over the past year, maybe more than any other year, is that it's important to do something that you really care about, that you can feel good about. Sometimes, I've wanted to drive the van straight into the Hudson, vegetables and all. The traffic, the needless parking tickets, the stooping over to make the bags, it can be a little much. But then Nicolle will tell me about a compliment we've gotten, or I'll give a doorman an unexpected watermelon and get back an unsolicited smile. A customer will tell us how she's lost ten pounds and feels great. A taxi will let me by, someone will laugh at my joke, the van will smell like bread, grapes, and rosemary, and I'll realize just how lucky I am. The sun will shine on Nicolle's face, the radio will play just the right songs, the sunflowers will bob their heads, the lights on Tenth Avenue will all turn green, the air through the window will feel cool against my skin, and I'll remember how beautiful the world, New York, can be.

It's Tuesday night, now, and I just spoke to my brother on the phone. I heard him call to Ramiro to count out the turnips *for us. I pictured the phone cradled between his face and shoulder as he put my acorn squash into wooden onion crates while we spoke. His hands might still be wet from mixing the mesclun. Later tonight, he'll be loading up the truck for market. The lights on the side of the barn will be on, and he'll probably be listening to some old Van Morrison or Bob Dylan tape of his. My sister will be over early in the morning to drive the truck down to Union Square. On Thursday, we'll all be over at her house, Nicolle, me, some of our friends, and my beautiful, wacky family, to say thanks for another year on Earth. During the winter, Nicolle will be auditioning, and working on her movie. I'll be finishing that *#@#* book and maybe starting another. Look for it in June. Might be looking for a new farm, I think, too. Anyone interested in being a partner? Long hours and short pay. All the root vegetables you can eat, though. Lettuce know. Have a great winter! Thanks, all, it's been a good season. We'll see you in the spring.*

VERBENA CRÈME BRÛLÉE
WITH LACE COOKIES

(VERBENA)

Serves 6 to 8

3 cups heavy cream

1 cup milk

¼ vanilla bean, split

1 tea bag of lemon verbena or

    ¼ cup fresh leaves

½ cup sugar

9 egg yolks

Preheat oven to 300 degrees.

In a saucepan, add the cream, milk, vanilla bean, lemon verbena, and ¼ cup sugar. Heat the mixture until a skin forms on top, but do not let it boil. Remove from the heat and let the mixture steep for about 1 hour.

In a large bowl, whisk the egg yolks with the remaining sugar. Reheat the cream mixture until warm. Slowly whisk the warm cream mixture into the egg yolks. Return the mixture to the saucepan and cook over a low heat, stirring constantly with a wooden spoon. Heat until the mixture thickens, about 10 minutes.

Strain the mixture through a fine mesh strainer into a bowl that sits in an ice bath. Fill the crème brûlée ramekins, or teacups, ¾ full of custard. Place ramekins in an ovenproof casserole dish and fill with water until halfway up sides to form water bath. Bake for 30 to 45 minutes or until set when moved from side to side. Cool before serving.

LACE COOKIES

1 pound melted butter	*pinch of vanilla*
2 cups sugar	*½ cup cream*
½ cup flour	*8 ounces chopped almonds*

Preheat oven to 400 degrees.

Melt butter in a saucepan. Whisk in the sugar and flour. Add the vanilla and cream. On a lightly buttered sheet pan, preferably Teflon, drop 1 tablespoon of batter every 2 inches apart until sheet pan is covered. Bake until slightly brown in color, about 6 to 8 minutes. Let cool until firm enough to handle. Cookies can be draped loosely over rolling pin for curved shape.

MAPLE TOFU WHIP

Yields 1 quart

4 tablespoons agar flakes

1 cup cold water

2 tablespoons arrowroot powder

1 cup soy milk

1 pound soft tofu

½ cup canola oil

½ cup maple syrup

2 tablespoons vanilla extract

1 tablespoon lemon juice

¼ teaspoon sea salt

In a heavy-bottomed saucepan, combine the agar flakes and cold water. Stir over medium flame and bring to a boil.

In a separate bowl, combine the arrowroot and soy milk, mix well, and add to boiling liquid. Cook liquid, stirring continuously, until the mixture begins to bubble. Remove from heat. Combine the cooked liquid with the tofu, oil, maple syrup, vanilla, lemon juice, and sea salt. Place in a food processor fitted with a steel blade and process until creamy. Pour into a container, cover, and place in the refrigerator for about 1 hour or until firm. Rewhip in the food processor before serving.

LEMON RAISIN KANTEN

(ANGELICA KITCHEN)

Serves 4

1 quart apple cider (can be substituted with pear juice)

¼ cup agar flakes

⅓ cup raisins

3 2-inch pieces (about ½ inch wide) lemon peel

1 tablespoon kuzu (can be substituted with arrowroot)

1 tablespoon cold water

1½ tablespoons fresh lemon juice, strained

In a 3-quart saucepan, combine the apple cider, agar flakes, raisins, and lemon peel. Bring to a simmer and cook gently for 5 minutes or until the agar flakes have dissolved. In a small bowl, combine the kuzu and cold water; mix well. Whisk the kuzu mixture into the pot and simmer for 1 minute. Remove from the heat and discard the lemon peel. Stir in the lemon juice. Pour the kanten into a Pyrex dish (minimum 2-quart capacity). Refrigerate. Allow kanten to cool before serving.

BERRY CLAFOUTI WITH CRÈME FRAÎCHE

(JUDSON GRILL)

2 eggs

⅓ cup sugar

½ vanilla bean, split and scraped

3 tablespoons flour

pinch salt

⅓ cup milk

⅔ cup crème fraîche or fresh
  whipped cream

1 pint mixed berries (strawberries,
  blueberries, raspberries,
  blackberries)

1 tablespoon confectioner's sugar,
  plus extra for dusting

Preheat oven to 375 degrees.

Whisk together the eggs and sugar until frothy. Add vanilla specks, flour, and salt. Mix until incorporated. Fold in the milk and ½ the crème fraîche. Spray a 10-inch nonstick pan with vegetable spray. Pour ⅓ of the batter into the pan. Bake in the oven for 3 minutes, just until the batter sets. Remove the pan from the oven and spread the mixed berries on as the next layer. Pour the remaining batter over the berries. Return the pan to the oven and continue baking for 12 to 16 minutes, or until the edges start to brown and the middle rises. Take out and let cool 20 minutes. Mix the remaining ⅓ cup of crème fraîche with the confectioner's sugar.

Cut the clafouti into 4 to 6 wedges, dust with the extra confectioner's sugar, and serve with the remaining berries and sweetened crème fraîche.

PECORINO ROMANO CON MIELE

(PECORINO ROMANO WITH HONEY)

(FELIDIA)

Serves 4

3 tablespoons thyme honey

½ pound Pecorino Romano

fresh grapes, figs, or orange zest for garnish

Warm the honey in a double boiler. Set chunks of freshly cut Pecorino Romano on a plate and drizzle with the warm honey. Decorate with fresh grapes, figs, or thin orange zest, and serve.

WILD RICE PUDDING

Serves 6 to 8

2 cups milk

1 cup half and half

1 cup heavy cream

½ cup sugar

½ cup white rice

½ cup wild rice

½ cup raisins

cinnamon and toasted sliced

   almonds for garnish

Combine milk, half and half, and cream in a heavy saucepan. Place over medium heat. Just before liquid boils, stir in the sugar and white rice. Bring to a boil, then reduce heat and simmer, stirring frequently. Place the wild rice in a separate saucepan, and add water to cover. Bring to a boil, then reduce heat. Cook until rice begins to burst open. Remove from flame and rinse with cool water. When the milk and white rice mixture thickens to a pudding-like consistency, remove from heat (approximately 1 hour). Stir in the cooked wild rice and raisins. Pour the mixture into a 9-by-9-inch baking dish. Sprinkle with cinnamon, and chill overnight.

To serve, cut into squares and place in a bowl with a small amount of half and half or heavy cream. Garnish with toasted sliced almonds.

FLUFFY BREAD PUDDING WITH
PEAR-RUM SAUCE

(DROVERS)

Serves 4

This bread pudding stays light because the egg whites are whipped separately and folded into the custard last.

6 cups bread, crusts cut off, cut into
1-inch cubes

1 cup raisins

1 cup ripe pear, peeled and diced

¼ teaspoon cinnamon

⅛ teaspoon nutmeg

⅛ teaspoon ginger

Custard (recipe follows)

Pear-Rum Sauce (recipe follows)

If the bread is very moist, dry it in a 300-degree oven for about 10 minutes, being careful not to let it brown. The centers of the cubes should still be moist.

Preheat oven to 350 degrees.

In a large bowl, combine the bread with the raisins, pear, and spices. Place equal amounts in 4 buttered ovenproof ramekins. Pour equal amounts of the custard over the bread. Bake for 25 minutes. Spoon Pear-Rum Sauce on top of the warm puddings, and serve.

CUSTARD

3 eggs, separated	3 cups milk
¾ cup sugar	2 tablespoons molasses
¼ teaspoon salt	¼ teaspoon vanilla

Lightly whip the egg yolks, add the sugar and salt, and whip until light yellow. Set aside. Whip the egg whites until soft peaks form. Set aside. Scald the milk together with the molasses and vanilla. Slowly pour the heated milk into the yolks, stirring constantly so that the yolks will incorporate smoothly. When finished, fold in the egg whites.

PEAR-RUM SAUCE

3 pears, peeled and cut into ½-inch dice	3 tablespoons butter
	2 tablespoons molasses
1 cup rum (we use Mt. Gay)	⅛ teaspoon cinnamon

Heat all of the ingredients in a saucepan over low heat until the pears soften and the sauce thickens, about 30 minutes.

RESOURCES

Angelica Kitchen
300 East Twelfth Street
(between First and
Second Avenues)
212-228-2909

Babbo Restaurant
110 Waverly Place
(between Sixth Avenue and
MacDougal Street)
212-777-0303

Cendrillon
45 Mercer Street
(between Broome and
Grand Streets)
212-343-9012

Col Legno
231 East Ninth Street
(between Second and Third
Avenues)
212-777-4650

Cub Room
131 Sullivan Street
(corner of Prince Street)
212-677-4100

Drovers
9 Jones Street (between
Bleecker and West Fourth
Streets)
212-627-1233

Felidia
243 East Fifty-eighth Street
(between Second and Third
Avenues)
212-758-1479

Ferdinando's Restaurant

Ferdinando's Focacceria
151 Union Street, Brooklyn
(between Columbia and Hicks
Streets)
718-855-1545

FRICO BAR

Frico Bar
402 West Forty-third Street
(corner of Ninth Avenue)
212-564-7272

GRAMERCY TAVERN

Gramercy Tavern
42 East Twentieth Street
(between Broadway and Park
Avenue South)
212-477-0777

The Grange Hall
50 Commerce Street (corner of
Barrow Street)
212-924-5246

HOME RESTAURANT

Home
20 Cornelia Street (between
Bleecker and West Fourth
Streets)
212-243-9579

Judson Grill
152 West Fifty-second Street
(between Sixth and Seventh
Avenues)
212-JU2-5252
(212-582-5252)

KNICKERBOCKER

Knickerbocker Bar and Grill
33 University Place (corner of
Ninth Street)
212-228-8490

Pō

Pó
31 Cornelia Street (between
Bleecker and West Fourth
Streets)
212-645-2189/1-800-656-7592

Patois

Patois
255 Smith Street, Brooklyn
(between Degraw and
Douglass Streets)
718-855-1535

Pearl Oyster Bar
18 Cornelia Street (between
Bleecker and West Fourth
Streets)
212-691-8211

SAVOY

Savoy
70 Prince Street (corner of
Crosby Street)
212-219-8570

Seahorse Tavern

Seahorse Tavern
65 Marsh Road
Noank, Connecticut
860-536-1670

Union Square Cafe

Union Square Cafe
21 East Sixteenth Street
(between Fifth Avenue and
Union Square West)
212-243-4020

Verbena

Verbena
54 Irving Place
(between Seventeenth and
Eighteenth Streets)
212-260-5454

MORE STUFF

COOKBOOKS BY THE CHEFS

*The Union Square
Cafe Cookbook*
by Danny Meyer and
Michael Romano
published by HarperCollins

Lidia's Italian Table
by Lidia Matticchio Bastianich
published by William Morrow

Esperienze Italiane: Lidia
Matticchio Bastianich's
tours of Italy,
focusing on food, wine,
art, and history
800-480-2426
E-mail: shelly@lidiasitaly.com

Fishers Island Oyster Farm
Fishers Island, New York
516-788-7889

My Brother's Farm Organic and
Local Produce Delivery Service
212-615-6733